FORGIVING &NOT FORGIVING

Why Sometimes It's Better *Not* to Forgive

Jeanne Safer, Ph.D.

Quill
An Imprint of HarperCollins*Publishers*

AUTHOR'S NOTE

The names and certain identifying characteristics of everyone in this book, with the exception of the two clergymen and members of my family, have been changed to protect their confidentiality.

A hardcover edition of this book was published in 1999 by Avon Books.

First Quill edition published 2000.

Designed by Rhea Braunstein

The Library of Congress has catalogued the hardcover edition as follows:
Safer, Jeanne.
   Forgiving and not forgiving : a new approach to resolving intimate betrayal / Jeanne Safer.—1st ed.
   p. cm.
   ISBN 0-380-97579-3
   1. Forgiveness. 2. Betrayal I. Title.
BF637.F67S34   1999   99-24409
158.2—dc21   CIP

ISBN 0-380-79471-3 (pbk.)

00 01 02 03 04 ❖/RRD 10 9 8 7 6 5 4 3 2

For Rick

Acknowledgments

I am grateful to the people I interviewed for teaching me the many meanings of forgiveness, and unforgiveness. I also want to thank my editors, Jennifer Brehl and Jennifer Hershey, and my agent Jennifer Rudolph Walsh, for giving me the opportunity to write it. For insight, inspiration, and support, I am indebted to Judith Kaufman, Paul Russo, and my husband Richard Brookhiser, to whom this book is dedicated.

◀ ▶

Suddenly through the window was heard the sweetest of songs. It was the little living nightingale that was sitting on a branch outside. She had heard of her Emperor's distress, and had come to bring him the hope and comfort of her song.

"You heavenly little bird, I know full well who you are. It was you I banished from my Empire, and yet your song has chased the evil visions from my bed, and driven Death from my heart. How can I reward you?"

"You have rewarded me; tears came to your eyes when I sang to you; I shall never forget what that meant to me. . . . In the evening I will sing so that you may be glad and also thoughtful. I will sing about the good and evil around you which are kept hidden from you."

—Hans Christian Andersen, "The Nightingale"

Contents

FORGIVING
&NOT
FORGIVING

Introduction

A 20/20 segment broadcast in early January: As the up-lifting music swells, the avuncular announcer intones "And now here's a resolution for the New Year we should all make—forgiveness." We see a mother and daughter estranged for years kiss and make up, a couple after just a few sessions of "forgiveness therapy" (all previous marriage counseling had failed) holding hands and renewing their vows. Amid the gauzy backgrounds, the inevitable tears flow, the inevitable hugs proliferate, and the inevitable psychological experts stop just short of claiming that failure to forgive causes cancer and heart disease. They say traditional psychotherapy has neglected this essential element of cure and that studies show that forgiving alleviates depression and enhances self-esteem.

Several weeks later, on *Good Morning America:* A rabbi asserts that "forgiving is like taking a poison out of your body," and a priest agrees that, otherwise, "evil is recycled."

Politicians caught in scandalous behavior make public displays of contrition and speak poignantly of how their ordeals have taught them the importance of not only asking forgiveness, but of granting it to their accusers.

What's wrong with this picture?

All the hype is not entirely inaccurate. We all know people (often in our own families) who haven't spoken to one another for so long that they have forgotten what they were angry about, couples whose mutual resentments are etched on their faces, acquaintances so obsessed with hating or plotting revenge on their enemies that they have alienated us. I have treated many patients like them in my twenty-five years as a psychotherapist. But don't we also know others—mature, even wise people—who passionately refuse to forgive wrongs, or who feel, despite their best efforts, that they cannot without doing violence to themselves? Has failure to forgive destroyed their ability to love?

Forgiving and Not Forgiving proposes a paradigm shift. It challenges the conventional wisdom and offers a new and consoling perspective: that forgiveness as it is commonly understood is only one of many routes to resolution, humanity, and peace, and that reengaging with the past is the best way to change the future. It charges that false forgiveness damages self and society, and that not forgiving without vindictiveness can be morally and emotionally right.

The capacity to forgive is an essential part of an examined life. However, enshrining universal forgiveness as a panacea, a requirement, or the only moral choice, is rigid, simplistic, and even pernicious. Forgiveness by the numbers leads too frequently to emotional inauthenticity—a condition rampant in contemporary America.

Everybody has something to forgive—parents who failed, lovers who left, friends who deceived, and—often the hardest of all—our own actions. (Crimes by strangers are not intimate betrayals because they do not violate a personal relationship with the victim and will not be considered here.) Though it is a cornerstone of the Judeo-Christian tradition, forgiveness is not "natural," or religion and society would not have to lobby so hard to get people to do it; the reflexive reaction to being hurt is hatred, outrage, and the desire for revenge. While forgiveness is not always necessary or possible, coming to terms with intimate betrayal is, and that is what this book is about.

Forgiving is as charged and protean a concept as love, as deeply personal, and as impossible to create by will, so there are no instructions here, only reflections and illustrations.

The book begins with my own story. My interest in forgiveness grew out of my personal battle with it, as well as my professional experience as a psychotherapist. I have spent the past twenty years resolving my relationship with my father, who betrayed me in a shocking way when I was a teenager, and from whom I was bitterly estranged when he died. The process, which I understand only in retrospect, has led to dramatic changes in the way I see the world, and myself.

You will also meet an extraordinary array of people in the course of the book—including a murderer, a princess, and my next-door neighbor—who tell how they forgave or why they did not. Young and old, straight and gay, these fifty men and women struggled with betrayals ranging from the minor hurts of everyday life to terrible suffering at the hands of people they needed and trusted. Some of them made conscious decisions that they resolutely carried out, some agonized for years over whether to forgive, and some, for excellent or dubious reasons, refused to try. They describe their coming to terms in rare and intimate detail. Because forgiveness stirs such intense and often surprising emotions, my conversations with them were powerfully moving; I saw one of my dearest friends cry for the first time in the fifteen years I have known her.

When should we try to forgive or refuse to do so? What are the differences in forgiving the living and the dead, relatives and others, the repentant and the remorseless? Do attitudes about forgiving change through the life cycle? Can forgiving be willed? And is it true, in the words of Mme de Stael, that to understand all is to forgive all? *Forgiving and Not Forgiving*, grounded in the insights of contemporary psychoanalytic psychotherapy, provides a new take on these questions, which until recently were primarily the province of religion and moral philosophy. Now the topic has been commandeered by the self-help movement and by psychologists who have a covertly religious agenda. Most of these ignore or reject the critical role that unconscious thoughts and feelings play in forgiveness—a role that must not be underestimated. Forgiveness has been cheapened by overuse until it has almost lost its meaning. I want to restore it.

In writing this book, I discovered that forgiveness encompasses many basic human concerns—grief, rage, ambivalence, remorse, and helplessness among them. The act is full of paradox; the most archetypal Christian act of forgiveness I encountered was by a nonbelieving Jew. Since people define identical experiences as forgiveness or unforgiveness, depending on their personal interpretation, no one outcome can be recommended for everyone.

I was also struck by how many people, including a number who did not consider themselves religious, felt guilty or even tortured about not having forgiven significant figures in their lives, particularly family members; "I feel what only the evil feel," said a woman who could not love and never mourned for her hateful mother. Many were warned by friends, clergy, or therapists that their failure to forgive would blight their lives, or lead to depression or unbearable regret. This assumption demonstrates how deeply ingrained, without regard for individual needs or circumstances, forgiveness is as an ideal and as an imperative in our culture.

Like members of the clergy, many psychotherapists tend to assume that forgiveness is the only sane solution to betrayal; a colleague told me, "If you don't forgive, you're doomed to be a victim for the rest of your life." I believe that, while most people do need to struggle with whether to forgive as part of therapy, not every one has to achieve it. People need to be told that resolved, thoughtful *un*forgiveness is as liberating as forgiveness. Therapists must take care not to foist forgiveness (or anger or anything else) on their patients, but rather to assist them in reaching their own conclusions. Patients intuitively know what their therapists expect, even if it is not explicitly stated, and comply without realizing it; this cuts off the exploration and grieving process essential for real resolution, and leads to compliance, false forgiveness, and secret despair.

Not all acts of forgiveness are authentic. Only the genuine variety, which requires mourning and insight, transforms a life. False forgiveness, the product of rationalization, lip service, and denial, does not lead to inner change any more than vengence—which is often confused with legitimate unforgiveness—does. It has become a superficial and suspect public display that undermines the real thing. A self-righteous identity as a "forgiver" or an unquestioning adherence to conventional forms can actually prevent the work of real forgiving and estrange people from their deepest feelings.

I entitled this book *Forgiving and Not Forgiving* to emphasize that the struggle to come to terms is a living experience that, like anxiety, accompanies us throughout life, rather than a straightforward job that you can and must complete successfully in order to "get on with your life." Real changes of heart and mind are arduous, subtle, precious, and rare. Forgiving metamorphoses over time, proceeding in tiny increments, with fits and starts, retrenchments, and the occasional dramatic revelation or radical reversal. Partial success, lingering doubts, and residual bitterness and grief are typical. The process is always at least as important as the outcome.

I have discovered that the resolution process (which may or may not lead to forgiveness) consists of three essential tasks—first, reengaging internally with the hurtful relationship; second, recognizing its emotional impact; and third, reinterpreting the meaning of the experience and one's own participation in it from a deeper and broader perspective. This tripartite model applies equally to forgiveness and real unforgiveness (as opposed to vengeance, which is more closely akin to false forgiveness.)

I believe that the exploration itself, rather than reaching any predetermined conclusion, is the essential task in every successful resolution. What matters most is attaining a more three-dimensional view of one's own life, even if it takes the form of knowing what cannot change and why. Self-examination and fearless confrontation with the past lead to understanding and acceptance of personal truth. This, in my opinion, is the only genuine basis for compassion, liberation, and—sometimes—forgiveness.

Deciding whether to forgive is one of the loneliest tasks in the world. It is most often performed in solitude, surrounded only by memories, in dialogue with yourself and those who are gone, torn between the longing to understand and overcome the pain and the dread of obliterating its meaning, wondering whether to annihilate love or to resurrect it. I hope this book provides company.

1
Forgiving My Father

The Little Assistant

I have never visited my father's grave. By the time he died, when I was thirty-two, the man I had adored and whom I resembled, who had introduced me at age five as "my assistant" when I accompanied him on his hospital rounds and spun nightly fairy tales starring me, had become less than a stranger.

I know why it happened, but I am still unnerved and disturbed by my icy remoteness, by the seeming indifference with which I witnessed his weeping lament the last time we met that soon he'd never see his "little Jeanne Kitten" again. I turned away from him as he had once turned away from me, and I let him suffer and die alone.

I was my daddy's darling from the day I was born. "I told your mother that she had a little girl with big cheeks," he used to recount to me, "and I gave you special pills to keep you small." It was he who named me; my mother, convinced that a masculine name would confer a certain sophistication as well as provide a convenient pen name, had called me "Gene," which my father—thankfully—prevailed on her to alter to "Jeanne" with the "e" pronounced so that I had a perpetual diminutive. This metamorphosed into "Jeanne Cat," which became the basis of nonsense rhymes he set to music and sang to me most of his life.

I always associate him with music. He was a retiring, shy, and serious anesthesiologist when that medical specialty was first being developed, and he invented various ingenious surgical devices that he never bothered to patent, but music was his hobby and means of self-expression. Into my teens, the mellow sounds of his clarinet or saxophone wafted from his office in the house he and my mother had designed and built. I used to take breaks from doing homework or even from talking on the telephone to sit with him in wordless communion while he played standards from the thirties and forties. And although I don't remember actively inviting him to listen, he'd often stop by as I played my guitar and sang one of my innumerable repertoire of folk ballads—all in minor keys about unrequited love—which I specialized in literally as well as figuratively in high school. At dusk, we used to take walks together in the yard he kept well manicured, inspecting the trees, the little bamboo grove, and the fat roses he'd selected for scent and color. Sometimes at night he would fall asleep himself in my room in the middle of telling me one of his stories about a bear and his princess.

Generosity was part of his nature. Having been raised with unnecessary penuriousness by immigrant parents, he compensated by acquiring and bestowing the best of everything. He wasn't flashy or extravagant, but craftsmanship and quality mattered to him, and shopping in discount stores was against his religion. Whenever my mother or I couldn't decide between two purchases, he always encouraged us to take both.

Unforced togetherness reigned in my family. My parents took me along on every vacation from the time I was six weeks old because, my mother explained with grudging approbation, my father couldn't bear to leave me with strangers. Although there was undoubtedly the classic mother/daughter rivalry for his affections—he found it easier to relate to a little assistant than to an adult woman—as well as marital tension, little of either surfaced. Our mutual need for accord caused them to shield me from, and me to minimize, what I later realized was major strife.

Despite the rumblings, my parents were as affectionate and playful with each other as they were with me. My mother's vivid liveliness complemented my father's wry introversion. Both had a need for harmony that forced conflicts underground, but I never doubted—and still do not—their genuine closeness and mutual appreciation in the early part of my childhood. They gave lavish parties where the guests never wanted to leave, traveled extensively, and spent my preadolescent years designing their home with a natural division of labor: he created the clever, elegant fixtures, she the bold, striking décor.

As is typical in physicians' families, my father was my in-house doctor until I left home. I went to a pediatrician for checkups, but he was the one who took care of me when I was sick or hurt. He was the master of the painless injection and the constructor of the most intricate, comfortable bandages. Years of emergency room experience gave him the coolest of heads in a crisis. His hands could ease any pain; his calm, knowing presence could take any fear away; he was the one who always had the answer. For years I kept and used the boxes of neatly labeled drug samples he gave me, and to this day I am each of my doctors' favorite patient.

My father took his daughter to work forty-five years before it became fashionably feminist to do so. My nightly visits to the hospital with him, where I met the patients and staff, seemed incredibly glamorous and important to me. My father was so respected, his work—pain control was his specialty—so humane. By including me, he was implicitly conveying that I belonged there, that I could be both smart and adorable. Years after his death, I was visiting my mother in the same hospital, and a colleague of his recognized me instantly as "Bernard's daughter;" I inherited his facial structure, his coloring, and alas, his legs. His enthusiasm for medicine waned over the years, although his skill did not, and he warned me against the rigors and frustrations of the profession; since he wrongly thought I had inherited his facility with languages, his idea of the perfect career for me was the diplomatic corps—a line of work for which I was singularly ill-suited. I always wanted to emulate his vocation, and in my own professional life chose the emotional rather than the physical realm, becoming the next Dr. Safer. Despite his incomprehension of my choice, he was tremendously proud of me.

Ironically for a healer, my father had one of those bodies that torments its occupant his entire life. As a young man, he had been excused from military duty in World War II because of ulcerative colitis. I learned only recently that when I was a year old, a faulty heart valve was detected and he was told he would die within the next twelve months. Although the prediction proved to be premature by thirty-one years, he must have always felt at some level that they were all borrowed—particularly since he knew more graphically and precisely than any layman what was going to happen to him.

The first illness of his that I was aware of nearly killed him. When I was in the fifth grade, shortly after we moved into our new house, peritonitis from a perforated ulcer made him a patient in his own hospital for three months. I never took seriously the possibility that he really could have died; the invulnerability I imbued him with and the intensity of my need for him precluded it.

At the time I could not understand how traumatic this extra brush with death was for him, but I believe it engendered or exacerbated a profound despair, and further cleaved fault lines of a self-esteem already deeply damaged. Imperceptibly, something both died and was preparing to erupt in him.

His pills may have kept me little (I never did get taller than five feet), but I grew up anyway, and he had a much harder time dealing with a young adolescent than with a child who had sat on his lap, walked under the table because it made him laugh, and unequivocally gave him the adoration he craved. Our bond remained, but became more problematic as he turned more distant and uncomfortable in general. Without fully comprehending, I registered his increasing isolation, alienation, and disappointment in life, his disillusionment with medicine and with marriage. Though his motives must have been mixed, he always took my side in my bitter struggle for independence from my mother, as she turned increasingly to me for the emotional contact he failed to provide.

It was around this transition that I started keeping a diary, which I have done ever since. The first volume— with a picture on its white vinyl cover of an iconically smiling teenage girl in pedal pushers reclining on the floor, pen in hand, as the words "One Year Diary" waft along with the notes from a now-antique record player— was filled, naturally enough, with pubescent angst: When would I get a bra? Would stuck-up Sandy invite me to her party? (She didn't.) Did Chuckie in the chartreuse pants like me? (He did, and he even asked me ice skating, which led to an additional problem since I couldn't skate.) In the next couple of years I chronicled my first serious crush, my discovery of the sweetly troubling delights of slow dancing, and the ultimate thrill—getting into an advanced English class in which I was one of only a handful of girls. This led to my first boyfriend, who called me every night and, in a tradition already established by my father's bedtime stories, made up imaginary companions for me.

Suddenly there is an entry unlike any other. The handwriting, in a radical departure from the carefully crafted, rounded letters that were then my norm, seems to be disintegrating, almost unrecognizable, falling off the lines on the page. The sentences are ungrammatical, barely coherent. It is a voice of shock and anguish I can barely identify as my own:

> *What—why—what have I done to deserve this, what? I'm only fourteen—my life couldn't be that sinful. My wonder-*

ful mother, my father. Oh God, SAVE them, save me. Don't
ruin my life, don't murder my faith. Quiet her, make her
relaxed, well, *whatever it is out in the open, never again.*
Make this whole episode a short-lived nightmare, over now
over always.

I was in the ninth grade when this happened. Then I
only knew what I overheard, but I saw that my parents
both seemed to go berserk in ways in keeping with their
personalities—my mother screaming hysterical accusa-
tions and weeping, my father stubbornly silent, treating
her as if she were crazy for suspecting him of something,
and avoiding me altogether. Suddenly, phones were being
ripped out of walls and locks repeatedly changed—this in
the home where concord had reigned, where voices had
never been raised, the custom-designed world where a
seamless, loving ease had permeated everything. All I
wanted was to stay in my room with the door locked,
playing my guitar and listening to music, desperately
seeking advice and comfort from other fourteen-year-olds;
I had no reliable adult to turn to. At the very start of my
own adolescent turbulence, I was thrust into a monstrous
adult psychodrama, in which I was inundated while being
simultaneously excluded, onlooker and victim.

I learned only recently—because I had never been told
or wanted to know—what the impetus was. My mother
had gotten a call from the garage that her car was ready.
The only problem was that it was sitting in our driveway
in perfect condition at the time. Horrified, she'd called a
friend, who informed her that a young woman who
worked at the hospital was going around the city brag-
ging that she would be "the next Mrs. Safer." My mother

went through my father's papers for the first time in her life and found a bill for a purchase she hadn't made from her favorite boutique, a shop I disliked because it seemed too staid; the saleswoman told her my father had come in and said he was buying an outfit for his daughter.

A week after the violent scene following my mother's discovery, I recorded an incident that reflected the devastated loneliness, helplessness, and sense of panic I felt:

> As I was walking in the yard just now I heard a noise—a flurrying noise—and at first I thought a man was hiding behind the bushes. Upon further investigation, I found a small beautiful mourning dove struggling. In vain I tried to discover what had happened—it looked at me with eyes so full of terror that I couldn't bear to see it, and I went inside.
>
> Poor thing—it's there now, suffering—hearing its companions of ten minutes ago flying merrily by, communicating to each other with their mysterious calls. Why must all beauty and innocence be destroyed?

I don't know how they resolved it. Unable or unwilling to leave for my sake or her own, she must have allowed herself to be persuaded that his behavior was an aberration or an illusion; he had steadfastly denied her accusation. I was mostly relieved that the screaming stopped and they seemed themselves again; I edited out the strain. With the power of denial so particularly effective in adolescence, I went back to my own life shaken but at least superficially put back together.

My diary returns to normal, filled with entries worrying about the exams I was taking, passages from books I was reading, and a detailed account of my first real date with the boy who called every night, who put his arm around me at the movies. But what I had so devoutly hoped was the end of turmoil turned out to be the beginning: the initial intimations of my father's secret double life.

A year went by. I had a new boyfriend from the English class, less tender but more superficially alluring, who asked me out for New Year's Eve. I read Freud, Dostoyevsky, and Lawrence Durell. Influenced perhaps by my efforts to understand the events of the past year, I gravely recorded that I had decided that my "mission in life" would be "to understand and explore the human mind."

Then one afternoon I was called out of class to the school counselor's office, something that had never happened before. I found my mother sitting there ashen-faced. She said, in a voice she was trying hard to control, "We're moving out of the house. Your father is having an affair."

This time she told me all the details. She had discovered that he had rented and furnished an apartment for another young woman who was ostensibly his assistant.

From the hotel in which she installed us—I hated it and longed to go back to my own room—I wrote in my diary:

I have nobody to turn to in my despair. I know no answer. I don't have the experience or wisdom or foresight to advise anything. And most horrible, I don't know whether any of this is true.

Having obtained the key and dispatched the occupant, my mother did more than tell me what my father had done; heedlessly, desperate for an ally, she insisted that I accompany her to see the site of his betrayal. Years later, far less forgiving of herself than I was of her, she said how deeply she regretted this and her other catastrophically oblivious actions toward me, actions indelible in their impact. At the time I was too horrified and furious—at least as much at her for involving me as at him for creating the situation—to remember many of the details, but I was struck by how different from our lovingly designed home this other place was, and by the tawdry robin's egg blue princess phone.

Afterward, I wrote only one brief entry: "I feel old."

This episode too was somehow resolved, and within weeks we moved back and took up being a family again. My father steadfastly denied everything, categorically, even indignantly, insisting once again that looks had been deceiving. We went on a vacation, they gave parties, but after that I could no longer miss that something subtle was always wrong; they seemed, if I looked closely, to be going through the motions of a marriage, trying hard to persuade themselves and each other and me that everything was really all right, when nothing was.

One of my mother's conditions for our return, a misguided act of symbolic reconsolidation, was that the unappealing Spanish colonial-style bedroom set from the apartment be given to me; she deluded herself that she was salvaging something for me, she explained long afterward. I wanted no part of the spoils, but the atmosphere of denial was so powerful that I guiltily shared the conviction that my tears showed a rebellious ingratitude for this generosity, and it stayed.

When I turned sixteen that summer, my mother took

a trip to Florida by herself for the first time. I happily took the opportunity to spend the week with the family of an older girlfriend and her extremely attractive younger brother, but I was plagued by doubts about what was really going on at home. One night I took the opportunity to see for myself:

Since we were right in the neighborhood my friends took me home to exchange clothes. Purposely, semiconsciously, I did not tell my father I was coming. You see, I had to know whether the business about his having a girlfriend was true.

The front screen door was locked, the entire house lit up. The TV was on full blast, which struck me because he dislikes it immensely. I rang the bell, waited five minutes and saw no one. Suspicious, I was just about to go around to the back door when he opened it, clad only in a bathing suit.

I walked into the den. My eye hit on a garishly tapestried woman's purse. Dazed, I mumbled something about getting clothes and rushed into my room, wanting to search the house, the vision of that purse spinning through me. I picked up several outfits, ran out and back to the comforting dark of the car, and said nothing.

We drove back to their house, stopping on the way for ice cream. I wanted desperately to cry. My friend's brother, whom I told, made me a vodka and tonic, the first drink I ever had.

What devastated me far more than my father's actions was how he protested his rectitude—this time to me—even when confronted with the evidence, the sickening ease of his lies. Despite my fervent desire to avoid the discussion, he had no shame about insisting that I too had perverted and distorted an innocent situation; the two women (I had only let myself register the presence of one of them) were merely there to "dye their hair and do the bills." I felt I had to tell my mother when she returned, omitting the bathing suit, the drink, and the outrageous explanation. Witnessing her anguish added another layer to my own.

Once again they reconciled. As much as that disturbs me now, it relieved me then because at least I had the haven of my own room back. This episode too seemed to be entirely, uncannily, eliminated from everybody's consciousness. Once more we had family dinners and they went to the movies. My father helped me with my math homework and never gave me a curfew or questioned my whereabouts. To preserve the remnants of my connection with him, because I still needed to love and respect him, my hatred and sense of outrage went underground almost immediately. But what I had seen infected me irreparably.

In addition to the hideous furniture, I had also inherited a pert little white Renault automobile from my father's first second household, and this I instantly adopted. That car was my ticket to freedom, and in it I drove away from the sordid suburban scene in which I was involuntarily immersed, straight to the bohemian part of town. There I met someone older, wilder, and more dangerous, whom I couldn't bring home. Although I had no awareness whatsoever that I craved revenge, the arena I chose to wreak it in, like my father's, was sex.

My method was perfectly designed to bond and damage both my father and me. The young man I fell passionately for was gifted, musical, unstable, and unfaithful. I was so inexperienced that at first I refused to believe it could have happened, and fainted dead away when a doctor confirmed that I was pregnant.

Abortion was legal nowhere in 1964. Since continuing the pregnancy was inconceivable to me, I thought of going the illegal route, but what little judgment I had at the time prevailed, and I told my father. The old emergency room attitude I hadn't seen in years returned. Without ever raising his voice, or chastising me in any way, he said, "There's no problem that doesn't have a solution. We'll take care of it." His only condition was that I not tell my mother.

Solving my problem required convincing the State Medical Board that my life was in danger and obtaining permission to perform the procedure legally. I don't know how he managed it—that he had to "eat crow" as a result was his one mild rebuke—but five weeks later he took me to the hospital after school. The next day I wrote:

The operation was the worst experience of my life. I can recall every moment—the gown to leave untied, the huge orderlies, lying on the table waiting, my father's voice and the anesthetic, then the deathly blackness. Four hours later he took me to a friend's house. He was wonderful.

Though my father never should have participated in the actual surgery, I was both horrified and comforted that he was there. The immensity of my gratitude was matched only by my shame and guilt; I wrote, "I want to fall weeping at my parents' feet, to beg their forgiveness."

I thought I felt terrible because I had narrowly escaped disgracing them; I didn't understand that the real cause of my anguish was that I had wanted to. My self-punishing retribution had forced him to be My Father the Doctor once more, to take care of me, to undo his abandonment publicly, to atone. Why had he violated our home? His multiple, indiscriminate affairs didn't seem like love or passion, merely monstrous self-indulgence. My identification with my mother had been only part of the reason I felt so utterly betrayed; his disregard had broken our special bond. I was ashamed of him, so I made him ashamed of me. Secondarily, I wanted to punish my mother for involving me. None of this, of course, did I understand until years later.

The following week I took five exams. In a few months I graduated from high school, went off to Europe for the summer, and wrote my father a heartfelt letter thanking him for his "total, compassionate love that pulled me out of hell."

Self-blame haunted me throughout my twenties, virtually disconnecting me from what I had been reacting to, while his illnesses became more frequent and more serious, and his escapades multiplied. Once when I was away at college my mother arrived on my doorstep because she had discovered he'd taken a trip with yet another woman. Then I believed I was finally free, safe in my own place and my own life miles away at last, and I could commiserate without being sucked in. But because I had not dealt with the meaning of my ordeal, or still less with the complexity of my relationship with him, neither was through with me yet.

Details continued to unfold, eventually exposing yet another alternate household, this time including among the woman's ten children a little girl to whom he also gave lavish presents; I had just gotten a job to spare him as much of the expense for my education as I could. This latest assault barely registered with me, because I could not tolerate believing that my daddy, who had shyly laid out a sweet smorgasbord of Boston Baked Beans, Red Hots, and every other box of candy he could find at the corner store for my delight when I was small, had turned into a sugar daddy, compulsively providing cars, clothes, and walking around money for a cavalcade of interchangeable mistresses.

After college, I entered graduate school in psychology as I had always planned, and met a gifted, unstable, musical medical student. Five years into our relationship, when we were discussing marriage, he came home one night and announced he was leaving, adding unapologetically that he had been sleeping with a mutual friend of ours. The gratuitous cruelty of his informing me about this affair, which had ended months earlier, as well as my subsequent discovery that it was one of many, made me question whether our love had ever been more than another sham. "His coldness has killed my tender memories," I wrote. "Maybe this is finally the death of my naïveté."

I had, of course, never questioned his fidelity, although I had had a dream about my father soon after we became involved:

My mother discovered that all through their trip to the Orient my father had brought a Japanese mistress along, taking elaborate and effective precautions to conceal her; he even arranged for her to use a separate departure lounge.

When I found out, I felt horror, disbelief, and a feeling of disequilibrium.

Afterward I had written presciently, "This feels like a bad omen, but I don't know why," and inquired no further into the meaning of the dream or its relevance to my current situation.

That I whose life had been saturated with infidelity should never suspect that it would happen to me exposed the depth of my need to eradicate my memories. This fresh abandonment finally jolted me into recognizing that I was repeating my parent's marriage in my own life.

During that period I also had two other dreams in which my father appeared. In one, he told me that he and my mother had really never been married at all, and that for thirty years she had been pretending that they had been; I wondered which of them was lying. In the other, I got a package from him addressed "To My Darling Daughter," but the label was in an unknown woman's handwriting. My response in both instances was shock and disbelief—the same combination I felt at every fresh revelation, every new layer of deception. Then I dismissed both dreams as obvious and transparent allusions; in retrospect I understand that they were telling me something urgent that I was in no state of mind to heed.

Why did I need dreams to reiterate what I already knew? I could not avoid the obvious facts of my father's repeated and devious infidelities, but I had blinded myself to their emotional impact on me. Every time a new revelation was unveiled, asleep or awake, I was shocked all over again, which indicates that I had not processed the evidence. My dreams kept reminding me, calling my attention to what I dared not understand because I lacked the emotional resources to assimilate it.

My denial, while it caused me extraordinary pain, also saved me; it was my symbolic way of keeping the door of my room locked so I could proceed with my own life. In addition to mimicking my parents' way of coping, compartmentalization protected me by keeping me somewhat separate from the inescapable upheaval around me at a time when I had few other strategies. These costly defenses helped me stay sane. As long as they were operative, however, I could not even begin to come to terms with my father; you cannot forgive someone until you know you have something to forgive him for.

I wrote my doctoral dissertation shortly after my relationship with the medical student ended, and my parents attended my graduation. Though I was feeling depressed and estranged from them, I was still pleased when a friend who sat with them told me that she noticed that my mother had been happy, but that my father had beamed with joy when I was awarded my Ph.D.

My father had several heart attacks as well as symptoms of diabetes, congestive heart failure, and intestinal complaints while I was completing my psychoanalytic training and establishing my private practice as a psychotherapist when I was in my late twenties. He was also getting careless; an automobile accident en route to the presumably dismantled ten-child household landed him in the hospital. That he must have felt ever more desperate about his disintegrating health, and was snatching whatever pleasure or distraction he could get, excused his conduct not at all in my eyes, although I still felt sorry that he was suffering.

What finally shattered the remnants of my love utterly was a slight shake of his head. During his hospitalization after the accident, my mother discovered that he had failed to endorse a health insurance form, without which she could not get reimbursed for his monumental medical expenses. The company would not pay her the benefits unless he authorized it. When he refused her plea to sign, she asked me to appeal to him; I complied because her financial security was at stake.

He seemed pale and preoccupied lying there and chatted on about trivialities. Searching in this shell for the father whose devotion I had never doubted despite everything, I approached his bedside. More sad than angry, I looked into the face that still resembled mine and handed him the document. "Sign this for my sake," I begged him, alluding to our special bond one final time. Whether from spite, or pique, or world-weariness, he turned his head to the wall. "I don't care if I never see him again," I muttered aloud to myself on my way out the door.

A few months later, on the last night of one of my increasingly truncated visits, he sat down next to me on the couch in our den and began to weep. It was the only time in my life that I saw him cry. "Soon I'll never see my little Jeanne Kitten again," he sobbed. *You have no right to call me that*, I thought to myself, and I got up and went to my room. I never saw him again.

My mother's bulletins about my father's condition grew steadily more ominous, and I realized in some disconnected way that now he was dying. Not once did I think to go and see him, or consider that I might make him feel better. Nor did I think to introduce him to Rick, the writer I had recently met, who was gifted, musical, and, for once, sane as well. I didn't even register the pathos of the remark I later learned that my father made as he was being admitted as a patient to his own hospital for what would be his last bout of illness—how he hoped that this time at least the bed would be soft. He was slowly suffocating, waiting in terror for his breath to stop, and I wouldn't even say goodbye.

In my dreams, however, I was there. My father and I were having the dialogue that we could never conduct in person because I was too cut off and he too far gone for us to engage with each other:

From my parents' house, I noticed a huge wave brewing in the distance. A patient of mine told me he had terminal cancer. As he spoke I could see his body bleeding internally; he was dying in front of my eyes. My father, who was there, started to comment, but I turned on him. "Don't you dare deny this or say anything stupid," I screamed. "I can't stand the fact that he's dying and there's nothing I can do." Then I embraced my patient, openly weeping with and for him.

The distant wave was the force of my coming tears, then but dimly perceived; only in this dream did the violence of my reaction to my father's ultimate act of abandonment, his negating our tie by refusing my last request, emerge. In waking life I felt almost nothing, numbed to the enormity of both my rage and my imminent loss. Because I had split off my anguish about my father, and my helpless longing to assuage his pain, I could only feel grief and the desire to give comfort for his stand-in, while turning my fury on him. But by misplacing my compassion, I was also keeping my father alive; here, he wasn't the one who was dying.

The dream I had the night before he actually died did acknowledge that reality, but recast him as the wise, brave man I wanted him to be:

I was sitting with Rick in my parents' bedroom, where the floor had been covered with old rags because of my father's incontinence. An attendant announced that my father did not have much time, and said "he's going" or "it's near the end." That thought had actually crossed my mind the night before the dream; was it my wish or was I simply recognizing the fact?

My father appeared, in a white silk robe trimmed in red. He was naked and unconcerned. "There's nothing more they can do for me; my time is coming," he told me. "Death has been my companion and has been speaking to me, telling me not to be afraid, that dying is a job to do, to perform well." He spoke calmly and with a serenity utterly contrasting to the degradation that has marked him. I took his hand, embraced him and wept as Rick watched.

In the language of the dream, incontinence in the bedroom referred to my father's moral, rather than physical, lapses. The robe in which he appeared was a transformed, purified image of the bathing suit he had obviously pulled on in haste when I surprised him *in flagrante* sixteen years earlier. Because in my fantasy he was communicating with me as deeply as I would have wished, I could express the feelings about losing him that I would not be able to experience the full brunt of for another sixteen years. My love lay dormant under my hate.

The rabbi read a powerful passage from an apocrophal text at the funeral:

> *Honor the physician with the honor that is his due*
> *in return for his services*
> *For he too has been created by the Lord*
> *healing itself comes from the Most High*
> *like a gift from a lord . . .*

Was my father really due honor? I wondered bitterly. There had been no healing for him, or for me, at the end. His death was gruesome and wretched, but it was also a relief; honor and dishonor were so commingled in his life that they seemed to cancel each other out, leaving me strangely unmoved. I never shed a tear in the cemetery, and I knew I'd never be back again.

But I was, thankfully, not entirely devoid of conscious grief, because on the day after his burial, I wrote:

> *My father's clock, the one I gave him, is now next to my bed, along with a profusion of roses from the yard. His absence, his physical absence, is so pervasive. I know I don't feel it all yet, though my nights are restless and it's hard to be alone.*
>
> *I'm glad his pain is over and hope the damage heals, but now the emptiness, the horror of his agony and the pitiful waste of his life disturb me terribly; I need to contemplate them. Goodbye, my daddy. How little real joy you knew! You never had a real friend. We never really understood each other. I miss you and don't quite know what I'm missing.*

Rick and I were engaged within the year. He spontaneously took up and enthusiastically augmented my father's nicknames for me, creating an entire menagerie of
creatures for my delight, drawing cartoons as well as com-
posing songs about them. He made up for much of the
pain I had endured, and I felt grateful that finally I was
able to find someone who epitomized my father's best
qualities but whose fidelity and sense of honor were truly
unimpeachable. Now I was sorry that they had never met.

When we were packing up my belongings to move to
our new apartment, I came upon the cache of prescription
drug samples my father had given me over the years,
which I had stashed away in my desk and dipped into as
needed. Though many of them were long outdated, I had
kept them as a kind of totem. Disposing of them was so
unexpectedly wrenching that I wrote a poem about it, the
first clear statement of the full gamut of my feelings about
him in all their contradiction:

THROWING OUT THE DRUGS
Bottles with no labels
orange and green and yellow and red pills
pills for all ills:
his neat perfect printing
his double rubber bands
vials for terrible pain
most of which he suffered
with injection instructions
I am afraid to use.
dispenser of medicine
I never questioned
all the life left of him

in my drawer of drugs
the raw, wasted contents of his
dear art.
may my hated, beloved healer, my
pitiful, shameful
trusted father
rest in peace.

This was the beginning of mourning.

The Nightingale

Thirteen years after my father died I dedicated my first book to his memory. The impulse took me by surprise. I had been writing in the autobiographical section of *Beyond Motherhood* about my regret that because I chose to be childless my husband would never be a father, when I remembered, and included, a tender memory of awaiting the sound of my father's car in the garage. As I was describing my delight when he hugged me, it struck me, for the first time, how much my greeting must have meant to him. I knew, I wrote, that the man I had married would not only have entertained and inspired a child as my father had, but, unlike him, "would never abandon her, would sustain her forever." The compensations of my adult life, intensified in a moment of lost possibility, had permitted me to recover a portion of his love, and my own. His later actions no longer entirely canceled out his earlier ones; his pride and encouragement of me were as real as his betrayal. I saw what I owed him. Though I hadn't cried at his funeral, tears fell when I wrote the inscription: tears of at least partial reconciliation.

How did I get there?

Coming to terms with my father—a process I expect to continue all my life—has evolved subliminally, giving me only occasional glimpses of my progress along the way. It was not a task I consciously undertook, nor one I understood as it unfolded; my knowledge of my own metamorphosis is almost entirely retrospective, and neither straightforward nor systematic nor complete. Yet as I look back I can see the logic and understand that it could not have happened any other way.

Even though forgiving him was never my conscious agenda, I was painfully aware that our relationship was far from settled. Self-examination has long been my personal and professional credo, so I knew I had work to do. In that sense, this process, while primarily unconscious, is a creation of my will; I chose to face disturbing truths about myself even though they turned out to be far more shattering than anything my father did.

Grieving for him, for me, and for what we created and destroyed together, has accompanied the entire experience so far and will persist. Dedicating my book to him unleashed the first of my tears. Since then, the distant wave from my dream on the eve of his death has washed over me frequently during the more extensive exploration of my past that ultimately led to writing this book.

I have welcomed these tears, because I know that a sense of loss means love and truth recovered.

THE first indication of how serious the unfinished business between us was came in a dream I had in my mid-thirties, the only one in which he had appeared since his death:

I had witnessed a murder and left town with the evidence to escape testifying. Finally, I felt so guilty that I called my father for advice. He was supportive and helpful, concerned, calm and wise. I decided to return and face it.

This dream was a turning point because it focused my attention away from my father's actions and onto my reactions. I was telling myself something I had never dared to consider before: that I was as guilty as he because I had seen things, and done things, that implicated me in the "crime." I had indeed witnessed something shocking as a teenager—his double adultery—and I had "testified"—told my mother—at the time, so what was I guilty of? I had fled the scene emotionally by withdrawing and denying what was going on. But there was something far worse that I had concealed from everybody, which was that I secretly hated him and wanted him dead in retribution. His accumulated betrayals, culminating in his final repudiation of me, had in fact not destroyed our tie as I had believed; I myself had converted it into hostile attachment masked as bitter detachment and contempt. The dream-murder, which I attributed to someone else to disguise my culpability, was my buried wish to kill my father for what he had done to me, my secret pleasure at his suffering. Being just a victim was my conscious alibi; I was actually the perpetrator of my vengeful rage against him, of which getting pregnant was but one expression. Now I was willing to go back to the scene of the crime, to confront my complicity in the destruction of our relationship. I did not now absolve my father of responsibility; I simply finally acknowledged my own.

Curiously enough, recognizing my hatred mitigated it. Shortly after the dream, for the first time I heard myself referring to my abortion quite naturally and comfortably in conversation with a colleague. I no longer considered it a shameful secret to be revealed to none but my most intimate friends, or feared that it showed that I was crazy or unfit to be a therapist. I saw clearly that it was an act of vengeance, precipitated by my destructive wishes, which punished both of us simultaneously. Self-punishment was inextricably linked to punishing him; hating a parent always involves hating yourself because of your internal relationship with that parent. Unraveling this connection broke the spell of the denial that had enveloped me for years.

Accepting my participation in our estrangement converted the sense of guilt that had oppressed me into a sense of accountability that liberated me. Prior to my revelation I had been forced to justify my unacceptable feelings and behavior by blaming him for causing them; paradoxically, not taking responsibility had made me feel unbearably guilty, and had driven the truth underground. He made me feel helpless, and I hated him for it. My hatred led to vengeance over which I had no control. I had to express in hurtful actions what I dared not let myself know or understand at the time. It all fed on itself.

My actions were in fact more than merely reactions to what he did—they were initiated by me against him. When I stopped covertly blaming myself, I spontaneously no longer needed to blame him either. Then I felt sad rather than guilty, angry, or ashamed; forgiving myself, and grieving for my own conduct, was the crucial step toward eventually forgiving him. The process of reengaging, recognizing, and reinterpreting, of acceptance and self-forgiveness, was repeated each time I uncovered a new stratum of my hatred. With every step, I saw my father more clearly.

My revised interpretation of events may seem like blaming the victim, but actually it was my way out of victimhood. My father provoked my reactions, but he did not cause them; I did. I am responsible for what I did and how I felt, though I could not do or feel otherwise at the time. Knowing I am the co-creator of the scenario restores my sense of power and permits me finally to be the agent in my own life.

Taking my share of responsibility was not the only thing that changed how I felt; growing up had a lot to do with it. I started mourning for my father only after my circumstances had proved that the damage he had inflicted was not irreparable. I was fortunate enough eventually to obtain from other sources what he failed to provide. I had come to terms with my mother, with whom everything was always more out in the open and who acknowledged and repented her part long ago. When I had what I needed I didn't have to hold on to him in the same way. Until then, my hidden hatred kept me attached to him in an eternal cycle of blame, the mirror image of the love I repudiated.

Turning fifty, the age he was when the whole thing started, marked another advance in my understanding. Contrasting my life with his, I saw that my marriage was happy, my profession satisfying, my health excellent. He (and my mother) had nurtured me enough in my early years to equip me to overcome later devastations, even those he himself inflicted; he had given me a far better childhood than his parents had given him. As wretched as he made my adolescence, I had known rare joys as his daughter, delights that enriched my life as much as his failures undermined it; I had negated, but never fully lost, those precious things. Life afforded me opportunities to make reparations to him, even as I believe it permitted him to make posthumous ones to me. I know my new writing career would have made him almost as happy as if I really had become a diplomat.

In the thirty-six years that had passed since that frantic diary entry, I too had hurt people I loved. Life experience as a mature woman allowed me to identify with a fifty-year-old man's predicament in ways I never could have imagined. In addition to evidence of my own limitations, all around me I saw desperate people as trapped in their marriages, their careers, their emotional dishonesty, their character flaws, as he had been. Some of them had behaved at least as badly and not half as well.

My adult perspective also showed me that he never acted intentionally against me; the child of a cold brute or a sadist would have had a very different task of resolution from mine. Despite the devastating disappointment I suffered, I felt glad that I had had something to lose rather than nothing at all to begin with.

He had not regarded me, but he had never intended to damage me. His conduct, while reprehensible, was not malevolent. It was selfish and desperate, even cowardly, but there was no malice in it—toward me, at least. I hated him, but he had not hated me even as he betrayed me.

The incremental lifting of my hostility helped me see more clearly, and what I saw relieved me. I could now

begin to sympathize with him, though I could never condone how he behaved; I was sorry that he could do no
better. I realized too that I had more of an impact on him
than I thought; he must have perceived that he had for-
feited my respect, and at some level known why.

In charting my progress, I can identify a sequence of
insights that was repeated and built upon over two decades. The foundation on which everything rested was
my recognition of what he had done and how deeply it
wounded me—that there was indeed something terrible
to forgive. This step took the longest, because it entailed
breaking through the denial that had held my family together throughout the ordeal.

Next came ferreting out the rage I had buried beneath
my surface disconnectedness, of which the abortion was
a manifestation. That I kept myself ignorant of the motives
for my behavior made it no less my own doing. I saw
how blaming my father and justifying myself kept me
involved with him and prevented me from facing responsibility for my own actions. Hatred and guilt both diminished when I understood this, and I felt more in control.

As I came into my own, I started to appreciate what
he had given me. My achievements and my relationships
sustained me and enabled me to see his lapses in a different light, from the perspective of an independent adult
rather than a wounded child.

With each successive revelation I tolerated knowing
more about me, then more about him, cumulatively en-
larging my understanding and admitting ever more complicated emotions. At each stage, I saw him more clearly
only after I had come to terms with some aspect of myself.
The same emotional sequence followed every fresh in-

sight: shock gave way to distress, and then to sorrow. From and through the sorrow I recovered something else that had been lost.

Even after I had made considerable strides toward forgiving my father, how I treated him when I knew he was dying continued to plague me. It occurred to me in my late forties that my father had not been the first important man in my life that I lost; the psychoanalyst I'd been seeing for years had suffered a fatal coronary the year before, at the age of fifty. I mourned for him deeply and completely, and even arranged a concert in his memory; he, too, was a musician. What was wrong with me that I never cried over my own father? At the time I told myself that the one deserved my grief, while the other did not. Suddenly it dawned on me that there was something faulty about my logic, particularly since many of my positive feelings for my analyst derived from my early relationship with my father. Hatred proved easier to stomach than heartlessness.

My lingering disquiet prompted me to take another look at a singular dream I'd had right before my father died:

My father gave me a cage in which perched a tiny bird with jewellike feathers. I opened the door and it sat on my finger.

The image had seemed magical, and it reminded me of Hans Christian Andersen's fairy tale "The Nightingale," which he had probably read to me as a child. Then I did not pursue its meaning; I was in no mood to accept presents from my father.

When I reread the story in preparation for writing about us, however, the metaphor overwhelmed me:

Something was sitting on his chest. He opened his eyes and saw that it was Death . . . "Music, music," cried the Emperor. "Dearest little golden bird, sing, I beg you, sing. I have given you gold and precious stones . . . sing, I beg you." But the bird remained silent—there was no one to wind it up, so it could not sing; but Death kept on staring at the Emperor from his great hollow eye-sockets. The silence became deeper and more terrifying.

Suddenly through the window was heard the sweetest of songs. It was the little living one that was sitting on a branch outside. She had heard of her Emperor's distress, and had come to bring him hope and comfort with her song. As she sang, the phantoms became paler and paler, the blood flowed quicker and quicker through the Emperor's frail body, and Death himself listened and said, "Sing on, little one, sing on . . ." "Thank you, thank you," said the Emperor. "You heavenly little bird, I know full well who you are. It was you I banished from my Empire, and yet your song has chased the evil visions from my bed, and driven Death from my heart. How can I reward you?"

"You have rewarded me; tears came to your eyes when I sang to you; I shall never forget what that meant to me. Those are the jewels that warm a singer's heart. But go to sleep now, and wake up well and strong again. I will sing to you." And she went on singing. At last the Emperor fell into a sweet slumber, a sweet soothing slumber . . .

Unlike the Nightingale, I had never forgiven that my father forsook my natural love for a mechanical form of consolation. After I was banished I would not go back. I refused to sing him to sleep.

The love I withheld could have kept him psychically alive, or helped him die well. I, his little assistant, did not assist him when he really needed it. There was no compassion in me, only the last, lethal vestiges of vengefulness that I kept hidden from myself, masked in coldness, avoided or explained away. I could have eased his way, done for him what he had done for me countless times, and chose not to—that I couldn't bear to face. My final retribution was to abandon him at the end, and I could not forgive myself because it was too awful to know I had done so. Far more than my earlier hostility, my callousness violated my sense of myself—I refused the compassion I would extend to a stranger because he who had been the closest had chosen to become a stranger. At that time I rationalized that I felt awkward, that I didn't know what to do, and that he was hard to comfort, but the truth was I stayed away and never even tried. Only now, when I am the age he was when I found him out that midsummer night, can we finally have a tender, though forever unilateral, reunion.

THE last time I went home to visit my mother I opened the door to my father's office, which had been kept closed for years, and walked in. It is now a storage room. His books and office stationery were stacked on the couch, and his diplomas still hung on the wall. I opened the top drawer of the sleek oak desk he had designed and saw notes on the symptoms of congestive heart failure—doubtless a checklist for his own use—in the small, precise handwriting that I had certainly not inherited. There in its purple velvet-lined case the saxophone he kept so lovingly polished lay tarnished. Outside his window the shaggy gray birch he had planted for its unusual bark had grown so massive that its roots were pushing up through the driveway.

I tried as hard as I could to grasp something of him, not to lose it. For both our sakes, I wanted so much for his spirit not to have been destroyed or contaminated, for his life not to have been in vain or to be judged only by its end. I know I will never be entirely at peace about him, and do not need to be. Now at least I can remember him devoid of bitterness. As I closed the door, I knew—imperfectly, incompletely, with angst I may never entirely lose—that I had him back at last.

A friend just called me from the hospital where he was holding a bedside vigil as his father was "finally going down the short road to death"—a father who brutally rejected and misused him for years and only at the end of his life came to recognize his son's worth: a father no better than mine.

Once more, I felt a stab of sorrow that I had not been able to console my own father in his last days. Then I felt too alienated, too cold and cut off, to offer him the only solace anybody can really have at death—the presence of those who care. But now, finally, I no longer blame myself, and I feel no hatred of him or of myself anymore—only grief that I wasn't wise enough to love him at the end.

I know I could have done nothing else at the time, because I needed the apology he could never give. For being too young and too hurt and too angry to sense his desperate need, I now ask him to forgive me.

2

What Is Forgiveness?

T HE process of forgiving my father, which I have chronicled, has now been going on for twenty years; why has it taken so long? Because genuine forgiveness demands every mental, moral, and spiritual resource you have. Like love, it never stays the same, never ends, and deepens over the years.

Forgiving—defined in the dictionary as "to excuse for a fault or offense, to grant pardon, renouncing anger or resentment"—is hard, painful work that can take a lifetime. Intimate betrayal requires a special kind of forgiving. Damage done by strangers undermines one's sense of justice; betrayal destroys faith in love, trust, and honor. Betrayers have no regard for the impact of their actions on victims they know intimately, even those they love. This disregard is especially devastating, because it confronts you with the knowledge that, at least for a time, you did not matter at all to someone who mattered deeply to you.

Nobody forgives spontaneously; victims must make an effort to move beyond their inevitable shock, rage, grief, and desire for revenge. Unless it solidifies into obsessive vengefulness, the natural urge to retaliate will dissipate and either be suppressed or worked through.

All betrayals are not equal. If the tie was not deep or long-standing, anger can simply fade away. A friend of mine was date-raped by an acquaintance she saw only once. She never thought about forgiving him, only about dispelling her shame over her own poor judgment. Sometimes forgiving is irrelevant because a relationship ceases to be significant; I can now encounter with equanimity a man I used to dread running into since he has not been part of my life for twenty-five years. Deep, lasting intimacies are another matter.

Whether to forgive becomes an issue when there is unfinished business with a betrayer, undimmed by time or distance. Recovering positive feelings about the relationship, a shift in attitude described as "wishing the other well," is a measure of success.

Does anyone actually "forgive and forget"? Some believe that they must erase or compartmentalize, but others insist that remembering is the very essence of forgiving. "I'm not interested in forgetting," one man told me. "It would mean I didn't give a damn about the person at all. I need to remember what my father and mother have done so I won't make the same mistakes." Another said, "I only know I've forgiven when I forget—the act of remembering negates part of forgiving. If you remember, there's a protected harbor for resentment." This aspect of the process, like many others, is highly subjective.

Forgiving is often confused with excusing, overlook-

ing, pardoning, and reconciling. To excuse is to explain—
or to explain away—a harmful action by understanding
the motivation behind it, or by citing mitigating circumstances. This diminishes the perceived severity of the deed
without entirely exonerating the offender, symbolically re-
ducing the charge from murder to manslaughter. Overlooking minimizes the offense by arguing that the
betrayer was helpless or ignorant; Jesus should have said
"Father *excuse* them, for they know not what they do."
Neither excusing nor overlooking qualifies as forgiveness
because both absolve the wrongdoer of responsibility. Pardoning, not punishing an offense as it deserves for mercy's sake, is not forgiveness either because someone other
than the injured party can grant it; only those directly
affected can forgive in the strictest sense. To reconcile is
to reestablish contact after the betrayer apologizes and has
been forgiven.

Although Christianity and Judaism both strongly encourage forgiveness, the two traditions interpret the concept differently. Dr. David Posner, a rabbi at Temple
Emanu-El, a Reform Jewish congregation in New York
City, explained to me that forgiveness is "the central
thrust" in God's relationship with humanity and in people's relationships with one another, and that there are
biblical injunctions not to bear grudges or seek revenge.
Judaism recognizes exceptions to this general rule, however: "There are things beyond the pale, certain things
which if you forgive you contradict your own righteous
nature. These only God can decide; it is arrogant to take
it upon yourself." As for the role of remorse, he said,
"You must forgive if the offending person comes and
begs, but there's no requirement if there is no contrition."

In contrast to the Christian view, "It's not the obligation of the wronged party."

Since family ties are paramount in Judaism, I asked him the hardest question: Should a Jew forgive an unrepentant incestuous parent? He seemed troubled, even anguished, by the conflict such a desecration presented. "It's the horrible specifics where righteousness becomes difficult to determine. In Roman times, there were only three things that it was acceptable to martyr oneself for, where you were supposed to prefer death—idolatry, murder, and incest. Forgiveness is incredibly important, but the Bible also commands us to 'eradicate the evil from your midst,' to never forget. There is a tradition of opposition to absolute evil: 'He that is merciful to the cruel will ultimately be cruel to the merciful.'"

He left me with the thought-provoking but uncomfortable conclusion that the case is not always clear nor the precepts easy to apply.

In contrast to Rabbi Posner's troubling exegesis, an aura of calm, considered certainty pervaded the doctrine expounded by Father Richard Neuhaus, a former Lutheran minister who is now priest at the Roman Catholic Church of the Immaculate Conception in Manhattan and President of The Institute of Religion in Public Life, a foundation that studies relations between church and state. Both Protestant and Catholic doctrine brook no exceptions to the rule of forgiveness; "not to forgive another is to block the cycle of forgiveness to oneself," he told me. "I must wish you well being, and I must recognize partly my complicity; one is always called upon to examine one's own conscience." How is this different from blaming the victim? "Life is marked by a deep fragility, based on the utterly gratuitous grace of God. Each person must be considered a sinner who fully deserves to be damned. You don't muck around with grace. You must be reckless—even promiscuous—in sharing grace with others." If a betrayal does violence to your sense of justice, must you adjust your sense of justice? "To wish revenge is evil. That doesn't take the edge off the horror of the crime; you must, as they say, 'hate the sin and love the sinner.' The community of the Church sustains you; it is not just an individual striving." One undertakes this task in imitation of Christ, "for the transformation of life into holiness."

I asked him, also, about incest. "If the parent denies it, the child should pray for the parent more urgently." To my concern that this could be interpreted as putting the burden on the aggrieved, he replied that forgiveness required "a willing acceptance of an enormous injustice, to bear the sins of others. By taking it on, you become implicated in the wrong, but you do it also out of your love for the other. In a relationship with a parent, where there are natural bonds of responsibility, you should do all you can, and pray for the grace to love." However, he also stated that while one must always desire reconciliation, "If in the exercise of prudential judgment, contact will lead to bad consequences," it is not a sin to avoid it.

"Forgiveness is the refusal to become entrapped in evil," Father Neuhaus asserted. "You are only freed from the behavior of the other when you forgive the other." How then would he counsel a battered wife, or a husband whose wife continues to commit adultery? "To wish for reconciliation. It is morally imperative to forgive in all circumstances. If you're full of rage you pray for God to help you overcome your rage."

I was struck by how radical and how absolute was the Christian concept of love, and by the precept that since no one deserves forgiveness, it should be bestowed on everyone. I also wondered whether the goal of universal, unconditional forgiveness, however persuasively argued, was realistic or even desirable; is forgiveness the only alternative to hatred, and unforgiveness always contaminated by it?

Forgiveness is less significant in Eastern cultures with nonmonotheistic religious traditions; Buddhists, for example, consider all pain, including the pain of betrayal, illusory, and seek to foster universal kindness and compassion rather than forgiveness per se. But in the West, even nonbelievers are profoundly affected by the Judeo-Christian ideas about forgiveness that permeate our society. Secular advocates of forgiveness encourage it for reasons of self-interest, maturity, or mental health. The pre–New Age religious consider it a moral duty that is necessary to perform in order to live a righteous life and to deserve God's mercy. For them, revenge is forbidden because it is evil—and so tempting that there are powerful sanctions against it ("Vengeance is mine; I will repay, saith the Lord") as well as incentives to encourage the opposite ("To err is human, to forgive divine").

Until recently, the only people professionally interested in forgiveness were theologians and moral philosophers. Now they have been joined by psychologists and advocates of twelve-step programs who promote the Christian version without overtly religious trappings. Their point of view dominates current writing on the subject. The alternative perspective, which grows out of my personal and professional experience, promotes emotional truth rather than moral ideals, and does not advocate forgiveness under all circumstances. I understand forgiveness as not simply a loving act of will and sacrifice, but a profound and complex state of mind determined by personal history, disavowed thoughts and feelings (hostility in particular), and each individual's unique point of view. It is often far from total. The resolution process that leads to the many varieties of forgiveness can also lead, under less propitious circumstances, to healthy, nonvengeful forms of unforgiveness.

Religiously oriented traditionalists believe that forgiveness is a universal good, a task that can be completed, and an act of will that is under conscious control. Since the decision is entirely up to the forgiver, whether the recipient repents or deserves pardon has no bearing. One group of psychologists who espouse this philosophy has devised a seventeen-step plan and a set of instructions to expedite the undertaking. Their "forgiveness therapy" instructs people on how to " deliberately give up resentment while fostering undeserved qualities of beneficence and compassion"—although they do caution that this feat "can rarely be completed in one session." As in Christianity, the wronged person is to overcome anger through selfless love for the wrongdoer. Forgiveness for them is a virtue to be cultivated and practiced constantly, not a capacity to be exercised conditionally.

Religious advocates and their psychologist allies assert that reconciliation is an entirely separate action from forgiveness, and that it is always possible to forgive without reconciling. Forgiving, they claim, does not subject victims to continued mistreatment from the unrepentant because the relationship need not be maintained. They ignore the reality of family life, in which, because the parties must continue to meet, the distinction does not hold, and forgiveness can indeed perpetuate abuse.

Must forgiveness be earned? Is it by its very nature unconditional, or does the injured party have the right to demand acknowledgment, contrition, amends, or redeeming virtues from the guilty party? Most Christians and many Jews, and those who have been influenced by the religious ethos, insist that true forgiveness is unrelated to anyone else's attitudes or actions. A victim's well-being should not depend on an offender's unreliable goodwill; if the culprit shows no remorse, the argument goes, the injured person, trapped in the inability to forgive, would be forced to suffer twice. They believe that bestowing this "gift of humbly absorbing the pain" on the undeserving is the only means of self-liberation.

Nonetheless, many people outside the religious orbit—and, as I will show, many people within it—insist on words or deeds of recompense. "The day I forgave my mother was the day she said to me 'I was wrong,' " one man explained to me. "Then she became a person." Even forgiving the dead can be contingent on their just deserts, if the injured party determines that there was enough love or goodness to warrant a change in attitude. For religious forgivers, the nature of the relationship in its entirety is immaterial; from my point of view, it is the only valid criterion.

ALL authentic acts of forgiveness accomplish three psychological tasks. Forgivers come to see themselves as active agents rather than passive victims, cease hating or blaming either party, and recover positive elements in their relationships with their betrayers. This transformation happens in three stages. Through a complex process of mourning and understanding, they *reengage* with the experience of betrayal, *recognize* its emotional impact, and *reinterpret* its meaning from a broader perspective. These stages are often consecutive, but can occur simultaneously or merge into one another. Any one can predominate, depending on the personality or the current emotional state of the forgiver. The sequence can be repeated, refined or redefined over time, and even double back on itself; recognition can, for example, lead to further reengagement or reinterpretation, as it did for me. Any part of the process can be reworked or can take on a new meaning in different phases of life. Nonvengeful unforgivers undergo a similar metamorphosis, undertake the same psychic tasks and progress through similar stages of resolution, but stop at a different point on the continuum; they also no longer hate themselves or their betrayers, although they never love their betrayers again.

There are two general types of forgiveness—*intentional*, which is willfully* pursued as a goal, and *implicit*, a happy incidental, often retrospective, consequence of self-examination; forgiving my father was an example of the retrospective type. Both intentional and implicit forgiveness are equally effective, but people who urgently seek to forgive out of personal or religious conviction (or are exhorted to do so) tend to feel more guilty if they fall short of their expectations.

*"Willfully" refers to the forgiver's purpose, not the result.

I believe that the definition of forgiveness should be broadened to include any state of mind that enables a person to reconnect psychically with a betrayer and to change the meaning and impact of the trauma, even if considerable anger remains. This encompasses a far wider range of responses than the norm. The spectrum ranges from what people describe as "unconditional love" to "positive indifference"—from reunion and reconciliation (with the living or the dead) virtually devoid of residual anger, all the way to a state of mind in which anger has replaced hatred and at least some small particle of goodness is regained. Most acts of forgiveness fall somewhere between these points and qualify as *partial forgiveness*. In this, the most common type of forgiveness—though it is rarely recognized as such—the person has recovered positive feelings toward the betrayer, but continues to feel ambivalent. Anger need not be eliminated for forgiveness to be real.

Partial forgiveness differs from *automatic* and *false forgiveness*. False forgivers deny the anger which partial forgivers recognize and uneasily tolerate. No psychic upheaval, and no transformation, occurs in the imitation types, only lip service. I believe that many acts of forgiveness undertaken at the behest of external agents, including "forgiveness therapists," are inauthentic or superficial, and damaging rather than curative. The pardon unthinkingly extended to pseudorepentent public figures is a particularly egregious and injurious example of false forgiveness.

Like any other profound emotional process, forgiveness—even intentional forgiveness—is never entirely a deliberate action; a person can take conscious steps to become receptive to change but cannot manufacture an authentic feeling or impose it from the outside. You cannot make yourself forgive any more than you can force yourself to fall in love.

Intention may make forgiveness possible, but it does not guarantee success. Even the best will in the world, the deepest desire, and the most assiduous efforts can do no more than create a state of mental openness. Therefore, people who set out to forgive are not necessarily any more successful than those for whom it occurs serendipitously.

I also believe that there are experiences of varying degrees of severity in every life in which refusing to forgive is the only emotionally authentic, or moral, course of action. Real unforgiveness is a legitimate outcome that grows out of the same process as forgiveness. Residual resentment often accompanies both forgiveness and unforgiveness; it is normal and does no damage to one's character.

My own willingness to examine my behavior as well as my father's initiated the process of resolution that for me led to forgiving, but I did not control, and could never have predicted, that result. Had circumstances been different in my life, I may never have forgiven my father—or my mother—to the extent that I have. The only thing you can do is take the resolution process as far as possible; where it ends is out of your hands.

Betrayal is not something people "get over," even when they resolve it. Forgiveness continues to develop over the whole of life, and its meaning constantly evolves.

Resolving intimate betrayal, whether by forgiving or not forgiving, always begins with the recognition that hurt and loss are real and indelible. Though the damage cannot be undone, the relationship to it can change.

3

How We Forgive I: Methods, Motives and Meanings

TWENTY-SEVEN-YEAR-OLD Jackie O'Connor has the wide eyes, the dewy freshness, the combination of long-limbed coltish awkwardness and grace common among aspiring actresses in New York City. She has also achieved two things rare among her peers: a couple of paid speaking parts in plays, and self-knowledge based on her struggle to forgive.

Jackie told me her "story of a young heart." One night when she was twenty, recently arrived from Montana and in love for the first time, she had gone to her boyfriend's apartment while he was away at work in order to surprise him when he got home. There she noticed one of her love letters on her purple stationery lying open on his desk. "How touching, he's rereading it," she thought as she picked it up—and discovered that it was from another woman, who evidently shared her taste in colors and companions. "I'll never forget the sensory elements of that moment, how the carpet felt under my feet," she recalled.

Subsequently, she learned that this man, a fellow acting student, had slept with every woman in their class, including a close friend of hers. Everybody knew but her.

Jackie made a distinction between these two betrayals that I was to hear frequently. "I forgave the woman almost instantly because I felt her deception wasn't intentional, and that her fault was being unconscious rather than malicious—but he made me question my relationship to the truth, my own awareness, and my knowledge of character. I had shared privileged information about my innocence and my womanhood with him, and his violating that was devastating." Damage willfully inflicted by someone you have chosen to love is both a betrayal and a statement about your own poor judgment; the combination of shame and pain makes such actions especially difficult to pardon.

After this shattering revelation, forgiving her faithless lover became the purpose of her life. Like many victims of betrayal, she wanted desperately to profit from her suffering. Jackie embarked on a systematic mission to reclaim her dignity and her ability to trust. *Reengaging* with him in this way was her first step toward resolving their relationship. To inspire herself, she put two quotations together in a picture frame and looked at it every day: "Some day his life will become a blessing instead of a curse" (one of her acting teacher's remarks) and "Dressing well is the best revenge" (Oscar Wilde's motto). The first lofty sentiment never entirely came to pass despite all her efforts, but the second, more practical one—from someone who lived by his own precept—got her through. "Every day I came to the studio gorgeously dressed. It was the only way I could maintain my self-respect." Jackie expressed her hostility and her wish to retaliate—a normal and universal reaction to betrayal—through militant self-adornment. She triumphed over her lover by actively converting her public humiliation into pride in the very realm where he had most deeply damaged her; she "dressed to kill."

Recognizing the significance of her ordeal marked the second stage of the resolution process. "Innocence despoiled is replaced by dignity. This is my education," she wrote in her journal; "It will make me a good judge of character." Suffering becomes coherent and valuable when there is a lesson to be learned.

Desertion by a lover always evokes past abandonments, and Jackie's early life had been filled with them. The daughter of alcoholic funeral directors, she grew up in a mortuary alone or in the care of virtual strangers. "My parents were AWOL a lot—nothing dramatic," she said, with practiced nonchalance. When the family was living in the Rocky Mountains, Jackie's mother was often so inebriated that she forgot to pick her daughter up after play rehearsals, leaving her to hike home an hour at night in the snow without boots. "It bothered me, but I said to myself that I had to forgive them; they were my parents and I wanted to be close," Jackie explained. Automatic forgiveness was the ransom she paid for love.

Children with neglectful parents make their situation bearable and comprehensible by denying their own hostility, directing it inward against themselves, and concluding that they deserve the bad treatment they receive. Later, they reflexively apply the same defensive logic to their adult relationships. "At first I internalized his actions as demonstrating my unworthiness," she told me. "I worried that not forgiving him was a comment on the smallness of my heart; was I holding on to anger to keep him in my life? But when I realized how self-involved that thinking was, I focused on him, and saw he had wronged me."

This was the first time Jackie had not instantly forgiven someone she loved. She concluded that, in this case, not forgiving severed an unhealthy tie that forgiving would have maintained. What changed was her attitude toward her reluctance rather than the feeling itself. "I stopped believing that willingness to forgive was the measure of my capacity to love. This is being an adult." Jackie's new "three-dimensional" perspective, her shift from blaming herself to holding both herself and her boyfriend accountable, indicates that she has reached the point of *reinterpretation*, the third stage of the resolution process.

Until this turning point, Jackie's tendency to preserve relationships by automatically rationalizing other people's behavior had led to forced, false forgiveness with residual anger and self-hatred. Discovering her real motives helped her alter this pattern, and the new understanding of forgiveness that emerged led to other changes. "I got out of classical acting training and into experimental work. There I found a new community of people I could trust. My professional and my spiritual life had parallels they never had before, and that gave me faith in myself."

Jackie's ordeal did not lead to forgiveness, but the process she went through transformed her life and permitted her to distinguish between the forgivable and the unforgivable on her own terms for the first time. She converted her compulsion to forgive to the capacity to choose. The process, not the outcome, made the difference.

Compulsive forgivers maintain relationships at all costs. Their fear of abandonment makes them deny anger and suppress personal needs that could alienate others. This common type of false forgiveness superficially resembles religiously motivated forgiveness, but the motives and meanings differ. Pathological attachment and separation anxiety of which the forgiver is unaware drive the one; legitimate and conscious (though to my mind overly constricting and unrealistic) ideals inspire the other.

Jackie started off attempting *intentional forgiveness*; forgiving her boyfriend was her consciously stated and actively pursued goal. She decided to forgive, and then tried to create the emotional conditions in which it could happen. Like smiling to make yourself feel happy, the technique sometimes works. Although she failed to attain her original objective, and never came to think of her unfaithful lover's life as the "blessing" the quotation in her picture frame promised, she succeeded in accomplishing something even more important. Her relationships are now much freer of masochism and bitterness, she can both love others and forgive them, and she has alleviated her depression and expanded her horizons—all benefits that traditionalists claim come through forgiveness alone. The best measure of success is not whether a person forgives, but how she lives.

Every act of forgiveness is a fingerprint bearing the unique stamp of the forgiver; similar acts of betrayal can elicit entirely different reactions.

Many years earlier, in 1960, another young actress in New York also set out to pardon a faithless lover, but instead of contemplating his misdeeds and analyzing her responses, she confronted him with a flourish in keeping with her flamboyant personality. Tammy Kaye's career had started with a bang. An actress and dancer with masses of red curls whose energy made her seem much taller than she actually was, Tammy landed a commercial on her first audition and made enough money to support herself and Kevin, the photographer she lived with, for an entire year. His career took much longer to launch, and by the time she was thirty, she had been the chief breadwinner for eight years; she had no idea that he had been repeatedly unfaithful for seven of them until a friend showed her evidence and named names. "The night I found out I went home, picked up my toothbrush and my underpants, and left," Tammy recalled. "He had been it for me, the love of my life. I couldn't work, couldn't even talk for two months. I'd never been betrayed by a man before; you never forget the first time this happens."

It took Tammy three years to recover fully from her shock and hurt. She resisted Kevin's repeated pleas to come back to him, until the same friend who had exposed him intervened again. "He sat me down and said, 'You know what you need to do? You need to let it go, to unburden yourself. Do it alone and in your own way—trust me, the words will come to you when the time is right.'" Tammy's friend served the same function as Jackie's quotations; he consoled her and motivated her to *reengage* with her trauma. Tammy saw the need to master her anger, and she too used imagery to practice. "It was important to imagine that I could sit in front of this man and not want to kill him and not feel bitter, not wish him harm. I needed to go with an open heart."

Her solution was one of the most memorable performances in her career: "I called him, and invited him to dinner at our old favorite restaurant, a place I'd never been able to go since we separated. He was excited, assuming I wanted to get back together. I was afraid I'd dissolve, but when he walked in I knew he was no longer an object of desire for me, and I had only one purpose— to end it, because it wasn't ended. He'd never seen me so calm. I spoke very little, and put my hands on the table; the physical gesture was as important as the words. I said, 'For three years I've been carrying a burden of anger and resentment. Those feelings almost destroyed me, and I don't want them anymore, so I'm giving them back to you.' Then I pushed my coffee cup across the table, emptying my side. 'I wish you no ill, I want nothing but freedom, and now I'm free of you. I forgive you for what you needed to do. I have no anger, I have no love, I have nothing.' I got up and walked out of the restaurant. He ran after me, astonished, but I said, 'I have nothing further to say.' It was incredibly liberating."

Six months later, when Tammy needed a photographer, she called Kevin. By mutual, unspoken consent, he never charged her for the job—or for any other he's done for her since. "I've told him that he has the rest of his life to pay me back. I said it humorously, but he understands," she told me with a twinkle in her eye.

Tammy's tale of forgiveness is a touch disingenuous; it is really a story of a singularly satisfying—and nonpathological—revenge that evolved into partial reconciliation. Her pleasure at his discomfiture shows that she was much angrier at Kevin than she realized during their encounter, despite her protestations to the contrary.

Tammy's coffee cup was the weapon she used to symbolically seduce and reject Kevin in the name of forgiveness. Aggressively recovering the power Kevin had wrested from her was an important element in her *reengagement* with him. Discharging her anger in this safely masked way relieved her, punished him, and later permitted her to give him the opportunity to make amends; this new receptivity was her *recognition* phase. His willingness to participate allowed her to absolve him in earnest— though with an ongoing, if playful, sense of entitlement. Had he not reciprocated, she would still have resolved their relationship, but would not have forgiven him.

Revenge, in the attenuated form Tammy exacted it, had beneficial consequences for victim and perpetrator alike. Religious forgivers see only the dark side of vengeance, as though blood feuds or hate-filled ruminations are the only form this impulse can take. In virtually every act of forgiveness, hostility is expressed, not merely put aside; healthy retaliatory measures initiate more resolutions than selfless love.

There is no typical act of forgiveness. Differences in age, experience, and temperament determine how a person responds to infidelity or any other intimate betrayal. Jackie was a young, self-analytical introvert, Tammy an older, impulsive extrovert. The singularity of their resolutions demonstrates the futility of encouraging all potential forgivers to follow any standardized procedure.

ADVICE cannot create forgiveness in an unwilling heart, but if the conditions are right, it can galvanize a willing one into action. Jackie's framed inspirational quotations and Tammy's friend served this function; Rebecca Sachs, a fifty-year-old Orthodox Jewish lawyer, got counsel from a higher source: a holy sage.

Rebecca did not even realize her mother was an alcoholic—or that she herself was angry about it—until she *reengaged* with their relationship when she entered psychotherapy in her thirties to deal with her depression and sense of isolation. "At that time I had no desire to forgive her because she had messed up my life," said this warm, earnest woman who was modestly but tastefully dressed in keeping with her faith. Raised in a nonobservent home, she had converted to orthodoxy in her late twenties. However, as Rebecca became more deeply religious, her unwillingness to forgive began to disturb her. "I knew the commandment to 'Honor thy father and mother.' God didn't just say to honor them if they've been nice and sober." In order to "straighten myself out," she had repeatedly sought rabbinical blessings as well as secular psychological help, but neither had ever given her the peace of mind she sought. She even considered changing her Hebrew name, in accordance with the numerological adage "If you change your name you change your luck," but an important *recognition* stopped her. "I was blocked because benediction comes through the female line; in Judaism you're a Jew if your mother's Jewish, and you must literally be blessed in your mother's name." She saw that repudiating a tie is no way to resolve it.

Rebecca finally found help by consulting a rabbi skilled in Kabbalah, the Jewish mystical tradition. This compelling man with a long beard cascading down his black satin robe was "a real presence," Rebecca said with a lowered voice. "He holds himself in a very holy place. Because I'm a woman I sat across and three seats diagonal to him, not face to face. They don't tell you as much as they know so as not to influence you, but he could tell my mother drank. 'It's time to forgive her,' he said. I said, 'I can't.' He said, 'But you must.' I knew he was right because not forgiving was hurting me. 'What can I do?' I asked, and he said 'Perform acts of kindness.' "

With her therapist's assent, Rebecca saw her spiritual adviser twice annually for six years and began volunteering at a hospital. This act of samaritanism, part of Rebecca's *recognition* phase, had the psychological benefits the sage foresaw: "I met people there who couldn't control their lives any more than she could, who weren't there by choice. Then it dawned on me that my mother too had been a sick person; that was the intellectual beginning." Rebecca now *reinterpreted* her mother's behavior, which had originally seemed malevolent and powerful, as weak and pitiful.

Imagery also altered Rebecca's perspective so that she could understand and empathize with her mother. "As the years went by and I became more connected with God, I tried to picture her and what her life was like. I saw that she had no one to help her. My poor mother was so unhappy, because she loved me so much it really hurt her that she had hurt me. Now I've forgiven her—in fact, I feel so bad for her, my heart hurts for her." Her *reinterpretation* phase will continue for the rest of her life, as mine will.

Rebecca has set up a charitable trust in her mother's name. "Since her death, the only way she can get credit with the Almighty is if I do good deeds. Now every donation I make will be toward my mother's merit. That makes me very happy." A concrete gesture—whether it is a book or a memorial fund—expresses hard-won compassion and neutralizes vestiges of guilt.

However, even the most strenuous effort to abolish deeply rooted anger does not make it disappear. "I must say that in my dreams it still comes out," Rebecca confessed. "There are episodes where she ruins things for me, scenes of distance and frustration, and I wake up depressed. I think it will always be there—there's no way to wipe it out entirely." Residual visceral reactions to childhood pain in no way diminish her achievement.

Finding meaning in suffering is an important source of comfort and part of every resolution process; for the devout this means "putting feelings in a spiritual context." Rebecca regularly reminds herself that the empty loneliness of her childhood has had positive consequences. "I have gone through this so that I can grasp other people's pain. It has made me perceptive and understanding." Symbolically, God has sent suffering not out of neglect, as her mother did, but out of fatherly love, to "allow me to go further." This makes her residual sorrow bearable, even redeeming, and gives her a reason to fight the bitterness she might otherwise cling to. "My past still leaves its marks, but God wants me to get over it," she insists. "If I don't agree, it's my limitation."

Also, for the first time in her life, Rebecca has help she can count on. She feels nourished and supported by the religious community she has joined. "Having recreated my family this way, getting what I never had when I was a child, I'm not hurting as much. I have found holiness and completeness."

EVERY potential forgiver faces the psychological obstacles of dealing with the trauma, coping with rage and humiliation, and deciding whether to repair or sever the relationship. In their radically different styles, these three women each developed a strategy suited to her own temperament—a personalized combination of self-examination, imagery, assistance from others, and efforts to understand and to profit from pain. While the degree to which they dispelled their anger and recovered positive feelings varied, they all succeeded in expunging their hatred and converting their passive suffering into active acceptance.

The decision to forgive can be prompted by religious conviction, personal morality, or psychological distress. Intentional forgivers, who try to will their behavior, believe—at least at first—that maintaining an important aspect of their self-image depends on achieving it: a good person is a forgiving person.

Definitions of goodness run the gamut from the abstract "It was simply the right thing to do" or "I want to be the bigger person and have an open heart," to the religious prescription "I had to ask how Christ would act." It can mean emulating a wise or holy model, or acting differently from a disappointing one. "Nobody in my family forgives anything," Tammy said. "I'm breaking the mold." A man who instantaneously forgave his stepdaughter for cruelly rejecting him told me that his own father had borne grudges all his life. "I want to be the kind of father who forgives," he said. The daughter of dramatically immature parents declared, "I'm doing this to be a grown-up, not to remain a kid with childish emotions."

Adhering to personal ideals and aspirations or conforming to societal expectations motivates many acts of forgiveness; avoiding the opposite—feeling or being "bad"—is also a powerful incentive. "You can't go on with only resentment, fury, and frustration," said a man whose life had been mired in those emotions for many years. A young woman whose adolescence was blighted by her rebellious hatred of her family eventually decided that "To be happy, one has to not be angry. Anger is so exhausting, and so counterproductive." Forgiveness, for many, is the key to personal growth.

WHILE not every act of forgiveness is consciously planned, the timing usually has an internal logic, which the forgiver may not even realize. Years afterward, people discover that they have changed their attitudes and perspectives in ways they never imagined, and could never have anticipated or deliberately constructed. *Implicit* or *retrospective* forgiveness that is a by-product of self-examination has as much healing power as the intentional variety.

Henry Mann never set out to pardon his father, a European refugee who used to beat him with his fists, throw dishes, and punch walls, who had forced Henry to attend a regimented religious school where he was the only English-speaking student, and had permitted Henry's "loathesome" mother to sleep with him in her bed for years. Although they had reached "a tenuous truce" when the elder Mr. Mann remarried, "it was always thin ice," said Henry. "I would get into rages about how he had treated me, and he said I should let the past go, but I never could." Only his father's massive coronary at the age of fifty-five, which left him hospitalized and debilitated for an entire year before he died, made the difference. Henry spent his thirty-second year nursing his father every day, and he died in Henry's arms. A father's heart attack brought about a son's change of heart.

Physical intimacy provided the setting in which a degree of emotional intimacy and communication the two of them had never known could develop—a literal as well as a symbolic *reengagement*. "I used to massage his feet to help him sleep," Henry recalled, with tenderness and sorrow. "We spent hours talking about us, about our family, and what was going on inside him. His answers were not as important as the fact that he was open. It was an intense process." Taking care of his father gave Henry a different perspective; it allowed him to *recognize* and to *reinterpret* his father's character and their relationship. "His suffering enabled me to see him not as my father but as a human being; it helped us pass on to another plane. It enabled me to love him in a freer way than I had. I saw that I did love him and that he was a decent man. I haven't achieved total and complete peace, but I have gained substantial insight." The time Henry spent in the hospital with his father condensed all three phases of the resolution process and had the same effect on Henry as volunteering had on Rebecca.

The role reversal also gave Henry a chance to reclaim a part of his childhood that his outrage had made him submerge. "It comforted me to be near him as an adult— and even sometimes as a child," he said. "There always was a side of my father that was extremely sweet, good, and boyish, when his anger wasn't erupting." Their bedside conversations also made him begin to realize things about his father's own troubled boyhood. "It took a long time before I could see what made him who he was, how limited he was, how helpless he had been. He had no teachers—he was raised by a brutal father himself, and he'd been beaten, too."

Henry's recognition of his father's predicament did not cause him to excuse the violence, or to minimize its continuing impact, but it did permit him to put the man's behavior in a context where it became more comprehensible—a common theme in coming to terms with a parent.

Since Mr. Mann's death, events in Henry's own life have increased his identification with his father. "I've become a father myself, and now I certainly know what it's like to want to hit a kid—you're holding up the whole world," Henry told me. Regret that his father never lived to see him become a prominent architect is mingled with deepened—but not unalloyed—love, born of grief he can fully express because of their reconciliation. "Something happened to me in that year; it was a gift to me. It's not so much that I forgive, but that I understand." However he defines it, Henry's change of heart meets the criteria for *implicit forgiveness*; he recovered positive feelings, diminished his hostility, and left his passive, victimized state behind.

It is not uncommon for a child to forgive an ailing parent. The sense of mortality and imminent loss prompts reconsideration of the relationship in its entirety, including what was good. In the face of death, the wish to avoid regret for things left undone and unsaid can resurface, and sometimes what was bad seems less salient.

Henry's father's illness and his own caretaking gave him an opportunity to reconfigure the past mentally, so that he became the father he himself had needed and wanted. The situation also altered their positions—now his father needed him, and he was the active, powerful one. The father he had wished dead was dying. Ministering to him had the dual meaning of giving love and of

assuaging Henry's guilt for an unconscious sadistic triumph; compassion and empathy become easier to feel
when the person who made you suffer is suffering himself—a subtle, sane, and socially acceptable outlet for
vengeance.

A crisis in Henry Mann's father's life created the opportunity for their rapprochement. Beverly Russo confronted
her father at a defining moment in her own life—on the
morning she moved out of her husband's house. Though
the two men had the same first name, killer charm, and
tendency to drink too much, Beverly had never connected
these events until we spoke six months afterward.

Beverly's father was a figure out of a fantasy—suave,
scintillating, and hugely successful. She remembers
swinging on his big biceps when she was an adoring little
girl and thinking he was the "smartest, handsomest guy
in the world." As a teenager, she accompanied him to
parties as his "mini-wife." Her girlfriends, intoxicated by
his sleek magnetism, called him "The Silver Fox"; he
drove a red Mercedes convertible with a car phone in
1966. It thrilled her when the family went to Little Italy
and the solicitous restaurant owners, who all seemed to
know him, said "put away your money—dinner's on the
house." Even after he did time in the federal penitentiary
for armed robbery, she had trouble accepting that her darling, debonair daddy was a Mafia hit man.

"I was terrified when I first realized the truth," said
Beverly, a thirty-five-year-old art teacher, "even though
I'd always known that crossing him would be dangerous.
For a year afterward I kept every light on, and only drove
in the right-hand lane." Her own unconscious murderous

hatred for this beloved murderer frightened her at least as much as any real danger.

Like Jackie O'Connor with her compensatory couture, Beverly took action to master helplessness and horror. "I made a chart that listed where I was and who I was with when I felt overwhelmed, and I saw a pattern—that whenever I felt trapped I'd freak out." Anxiety turned to rage when she began to realize the extent of her father's betrayal. "Once the fear subsided I was very, very pissed off. He destroyed my innocence; I had never believed he could do anything wrong, and suddenly I found myself yelling at perfect strangers in the supermarket." As is often the case, communicating anger neutralized it. "Telling my story somehow got me better. I just talked the thing to death in therapy until I came to terms." The list, the fury, and the conversations were her combined *reengagement/recognition* phase.

The frequency with which forgivers use violent imagery underlines the pivotal, if largely unacknowledged, role aggression plays in the resolution process. "Talking it to death" served the same function for Beverly that "dressing to kill" did for Jackie. Allowing herself to experience her natural feelings of outrage at her father's criminality showed that her denial of his true nature had finally lifted. Discharging hostility in a sublimated form helps master it.

It was no coincidence that Beverly confronted her father and ended her marriage simultaneously. "Leaving my marriage made me less afraid of my father, because I'd been afraid of my husband, too; I had picked a man just like my father." Although she did not know it at the time, separating physically from the one gave her the courage to separate psychically from the other.

Although Mr. Russo reacted as might be expected, calling him was a breakthrough. "When I said it was impossible for us to have a healthy relationship, he lashed out at me like a wild animal; it must have triggered his own guilt and fear. Then he got angry, and then self-pitying. You'd think I would have needed his validation, but I didn't. Telling my father the truth was beautiful, it was eloquent—I was so ready that I surprised myself. That's when I began to forgive him." The sound of her own voice was all the validation she needed.

Simply venting outrage, as misguided therapists often encourage, is as damaging as trying to override it; aggression must be processed. The tone of Beverly's phone call was the result of carefully cultivated understanding and was part of her ongoing strife to face a shocking reality. It was a milestone, not a destination.

Forced attempts at empathy with the betrayer, another naïve and oft-recommended technique, failed for Beverly. "I tried really hard to forgive my father because he was a damaged child, but it didn't work; my anger just subsided for a little while. Forgiveness only came with acceptance in my heart. Until I did that, nothing changed." To accept on the deepest level, where true change comes from, meant knowing that her father was primarily a malign force in her life and grieving for the loss of the illusion that he was a benign one.

Beverly has gone as far as she can in accepting her father's fall from grace; contempt and compassion for her father are commingled. "I haven't totally forgiven him, but I've come a long way. I'm nowhere near as angry as

I once was. I accept my feelings of shock and horror, but now he's an old drunk who doesn't work, and I feel sorry for him. One thing I take from him is the culture he exposed me to and my creativity—he was very exciting," she said, acknowledging the aspect of his glamour that was genuine. "I'm tremendously relieved; I feel no guilt about still being angry at him. I did the best I could to reach him, and I did it respectfully and peacefully. The rest is up to him." There is sorrow rather than coldness in her voice when she speaks of him, the quiet acceptance very like completed mourning.

Her ambiguous resolution belongs in the category of *partial forgiveness,* an ambivalent state in which something positive is regained, but the negative is so powerful that it remains, though defanged. This is probably the most widespread and underappreciated type of forgiveness.

Beverly has even managed to alchemize her father's worst flaw, the felony he was incarcerated for as well as the others she dare not imagine, into the thing she is most proud of in herself: "I'd go to jail for causes I believe in," she told me. Even now, some of the Fox's old allure shines through the tarnish.

Not all attempts to forgive succeed. Jackie O'Connor began as a compulsive forgiver with a systematic and carefully reasoned plan of action. When she developed the capacity to discriminate, she decided not to forgive the person she originally set out to exonerate. Tammy Kaye eventually forgave and partially reconciled with her faithless lover after gratifyingly rejecting him with a grand gesture of "forgiveness." Rebecca Sachs, striving to follow the dictates of her faith and her teacher, did change the way she felt about her alcoholic mother, but still struggles with anger about her childhood, which she tries to transmute as her ideals require.

Forgiving can also be a happy accident. Understanding their brutal fathers, not forgiving them, was the goal for Henry Mann and Beverly Russo. Henry's reconciliation with his father would never have happened without their renewed contact and role reversal during his father's final illness. Beverly's efforts permitted her to accept her father's criminality even though he denied his guilt.

All five found ways to progress through the three stages of resolution—by constructing charts, putting wise sayings in picture frames, consulting various friends and experts for guidance—and saw reality differently as a result. Each has moved beyond betrayal in a particular way, though each is still marked by it.

Their stories are amalgams of unique and universal themes in the struggle to forgive. Personality and circumstances shaped each trajectory—how much ambivalence they felt, how much love they could recover. In some cases, the reaction of the guilty party made a tremendous difference.

People end up at different points on the forgiveness spectrum when they resolve intimate betrayals, but every resolution has characteristics in common. Everyone progresses through the stages of reengagement, recognition, and reinterpretation—often more than once. Each makes efforts, if not to forgive, at least to understand, the past. There is always movement from passivity to activity, intellectual revision of how the perpetrator's motivation is explained and understood, and an emotional shift from rage to sorrow. Even after we complete the main work of coming to terms, the relationship to our traumas and our traumatizers continues to change in direction and significance over time, subliminally influencing our lives in ways that always surprise us.

4

How We Forgive II: Forgiveness Through the Life Cycle

FORGIVENESS and time are inextricably linked. Recovering and reinterpreting the past takes time to bring about and changes as time passes. This makes forgiving a very different enterprise in young adulthood, midlife, or old age.

New ties resonate with old ones. As memory recedes and life progresses, traumas from the past are woven into the tapestry of ongoing experience where they become the background, rather than the focus. When people hurt less, they can think more.

Sometimes, though, the passionate importunity of youth makes possible feats of forgiveness no older person would risk. The young can have surprising maturity of judgment, while their elders stay mired in fear and folly. Conversely, self-knowledge born of experience gives some people understanding and open-mindedness later in life that would have been inconceivable earlier. The limitations that both sinned against and sinner face at the end of life can either expand or constrict their capacity to change.

It is often assumed that aging makes people more forgiving. This is not always true, and even when it is, not necessarily a good thing. Some older people choose to forgive one person and not another, and rightly consider this progress from their earlier automatism; they finally learn to do what is right for them, rather than what they thought was expected of them. Forgiveness is not monolithic.

Sophia Agnoletti, Jessica Kramer, and Dana Reinhardt confronted their private anguish at ages twenty-one, fifty, and seventy respectively—all important milestones and classic occasions for taking stock. The time in their lives when they took up the work of forgiveness and progressed through its three stages, determined how they did it, why they did it, and what it meant.

I had known from our preliminary phone conversation that Princess Sophia Agnoletti was a self-possessed twenty-one-year-old, but I was not prepared for her extraordinary looks. Like the exotic heroine of a science-fiction movie, she seemed to be two people spliced together. A natural blond stripe bisected her darker hair. Her left eyebrow and eyelashes were platinum blond and her left eye light blue, while the features on the right side of her face were brunette and her right eye dark brown. "My looks have always been a sign to me that I was put on earth for some purpose," she told me. That purpose, she believes with youthful idealism, is to change the destiny of her family through forgiveness.

Sophia has had plenty of opportunities to put her theory

into practice. The daughter of a Spanish noblewoman and a playboy who was the black sheep of a titled family of Italian industrialists, she was raised by maids on three continents, flunked out of various private schools, and had seen and done it all by the time she was eighteen. Her father's exploits with drugs and women are notorious even among his peers and the frequent subject of international press attention; recently she found herself at a party with one of his current flames, a girl her own age. "He not only allowed me to be exposed to this, but honestly feels it's okay. I'm still angry about it—I think it's disgusting and inexcusable. I used to be the only adult in my family, but he's more grown-up now—he acts about fifteen," she said of this sixty-year-old man with more irony than bitterness.

When she herself was fifteen, Sophia loathed her father and took up his vices with a vengeance, simultaneously rebelling against him and identifying with him. "I was doing in my teens what he was doing at forty—promiscuous sex and coke every night," she recalled. But unlike her father, Sophia entered therapy and started attending Narcotics Anonymous at seventeen. "I was miserable and furious, but then I sorted through my whole childhood. I learned not to lie or hide my feelings." Sophia has molded herself into the obverse of her father's image; "his worst qualities are my best qualities," she stated matter-of-factly.

Her new understanding led her to move back home to live with him while she finishes college. Sophia's need for family ties is so strong that she willingly overlooks impediments that might seem insurmountable to someone else. "I do wonder sometimes why I tell him I love him, because he can be so heartless and thoughtless. His own parents never showed him any love. His behavior is bad, but his soul isn't bad—you can see by the way he speaks that he's a poor, sweet little kid who doesn't know any better; I pity his suffering." As is typical of children who are more mature than their parents, she has herself become the parent she needed, and derives nurturance by providing it.

Sophia's compassion is a self-enhancing, conscious choice, rather than the reflexive behavior more common at her age. She does not deny her father's flaws but knows there is more to him.

It has been an enormous relief for Sophia to realize that her father's antics stem from his own personality and history, and that she had nothing to do with it. "As a child I thought that all this stuff was my fault, but now I know that he was too much of a child to take care of his own child. I decided that if he's not going to face himself, I'm going to be the one to change this. Maybe I can tell my father he's good—nobody has—even if he doesn't listen. I feel I should take care of him—see him, do things with him, be a better parent to him than he had." A reclamation project to which someone older might react cynically or see as burdensome, a young woman embraces with optimistic energy.

Zeal like Sophia's is not necessarily naïve. Even though her father has never made amends directly, she senses his goodwill, and appreciates his genuinely redeeming features. "There's not a nasty bone in his body— he's a really kind, good man who doesn't know the first thing about himself." His loyalty, she trusts, will never let her down; it is the one thing that justifies tolerating everything else. "I know my family are the only people who will love me no matter what I do. One has to suck it up sometimes even if they aren't capable of apologizing; they are your own people, and they'll stick by you more than anybody else will."

Sophia's exotic face symbolizes the goal she has given herself. "My appearance is part of who I am, and I'm here for a reason. I have a destiny to set things straight, to find the goodness in everything." Her current heightened sense of power compensates for her years of helplessness and emotional deprivation in the midst of wealth.

Part of her message has gotten through. "My father treats me with respect now, almost like a peer. He has a feeling that I know what's going on." With the honesty she prides herself on, she acknowledges the mixture of loving sympathy and gratifying superiority she feels. "I know it sounds awful, but I've surpassed my father. I can see that he's a little boy in a big body. My spirit is greater than his and he can't not see that. I dominate the family now. I love everything about it, even the bad things. It's so worthwhile to really work this through and get over being angry."

Sustaining a bond with so trying a father involves overlooking a great deal. She has learned to tolerate his somewhat tempered but still extensive carousing, and to recognize the limits of her influence. She manages this difficult task—a common one for people who have reconciled with loved ones who continue to behave badly—with sensitivity. "My anger still comes out, but humorously now. And I don't discuss his drinking—it bothers me, but we're all allowed to numb our pain, and the lucky thing is that he's the nicest drunk you've ever met. I know he's weak and cowardly but I don't want to dwell on his bad points."

Despite the toll on her, Sophia considers forgiving her father a blessing that she brought about by force of character, the proudest accomplishment of her life. "It was terribly painful to deal with him—I had to relive everything. It's awful but it's great, and once you get some distance you wonder why you didn't do it before and you want to keep doing it." There is no doubt in her mind that forgiving him gave her more than it cost her. "If people are decent—even if their best wasn't much—to forgive them makes you more powerful." Her attitude springs from youthful idealism, as well as from her need to show that she is mature, responsible, and in control.

Calling attention to her moral superiority is a natural, relatively mild, expression of hostility toward her father that does not disqualify Sophia from having genuinely forgiven him. It is clearly only part of what she feels— and has the added advantage of being true. "I'm in a hurry to do things. I had to come out of the awful state my life was in; I couldn't grow up until I'd dealt with him, and I knew I'd be like him until I did. One has to want to forgive one's family—if you want to hate them then you will. It's the stronger, luckier people who figure this out."

Forgiving her father was clearly a wise move for Sophia; was it the best thing for someone in her position to do? In a case like this, I believe it is. The daughter saw that something in her father deserved her devotion and that, despite his conduct, he loved her dearly. She had the good fortune to discover this early in life and was grateful that she could. Reconciling is warranted when weakness, rather than coldness or malice, causes appalling behavior. Sophia's father was capable of tenderness and loyalty; a warm heart lay buried beneath his debauchery and neglect. When there is mutual love to be resuscitated, it is always in one's interest to make the effort.

Sᴏᴘʜɪᴀ Agnoletti forgave her father in order to become an adult; behavioral science writer Jessica Kramer could not forgive hers until she had fully become one herself. Jessica was Sophia Agnoletti's age when she came home from college one weekend more out of duty than desire, to find an ambulance and a crowd of police cars in front of her house. Her father had asphyxiated himself in the garage two hours before she arrived. "If I hadn't started late because I didn't want to go there I would have been the one to find his body," she said in the emotionally flat tone, which until recently was her only way of coping with the horror.

Jessica's father had been the source of much of her emotional sustenance throughout her life; her mother was an unnaturally cold, self-involved woman who had alienated her daughter as well as her husband. Jessica had actually been relieved to discover that her father was in love with another woman and was furious that he stayed in a marriage as destructive to her own happiness as it was to his. "At that time in my life I didn't realize what was really going on; I thought it was a betrayal of me that he didn't leave and stop submitting me to their awful relationship."

Shortly before he died, Jessica got an accusatory letter from her father that devastated her in retrospect. " 'I'll never know you and you'll never know me,' he wrote, and it was true; I was escaping from him. He knew I thought he was a coward, and I was also scared and angry that he was deteriorating emotionally. My solution was to stay away and retreat into my life at college. He abandoned me, but I also abandoned him."

Jessica never shed a tear at the funeral, nor for ten years afterward. "I knew it was strange, but I was very closed off. I had to handle it on my own." She also unconsciously punished herself for failing her father by leaving her devoted boyfriend and giving up a chance to attend a prestigious graduate program. "It was self-destructive to give up everything I loved—I became totally lost because I felt so guilty that he said I didn't understand him, and I knew I didn't want to."

Only much later did Jessica recall how much her father had doted on her and begin to mourn him. "I realized I bought myself extravagant treats just like he used to do for me even though money was always scarce, and then I cried. I was so mad that he had rejected whatever kind gesture I tried to make in the last year of his life, and so disturbed that I had rejected him, that I never really admitted how much he abandoned me when he killed himself." Recognizing the depth of her loss, the legitimacy of her reactions, and the limitations that prevented solace and communication between them slowly allowed her to recover the power of their mutual love.

Now Jessica is the same age her father was when he took his life and irreparably altered hers. "His suicide changed everything for me. I threw away my life, but then I found another one. If it hadn't happened, I probably never would have become psychologically minded or have chosen this career." Like many people who have successfully forgiven, Jessica sees the positive effects without denying the terrible ones. "The anger has changed into an ache," she said, crying a little at the thought.

As a mature adult herself, Jessica can feel more sympathy for both her father and herself. "I was being called upon to act more mature than my years. I felt I didn't rise to the occasion, but now I'm aware that that's all right; my immaturity couldn't be helped. In some ways I was very mature. I didn't have the experience of long-term relationships and I had no idea how hard it is to leave one. These are things I would have had to be a lot older to grasp. It's also understandable that I rejected him. I had to avoid going back into the abyss of hate and more hate that was his marriage. To ask me to have been sympathetic that he had to stay there was much more than I could possibly have borne. Maybe I could now at fifty, but I'm not even sure of that."

Time and experience have altered Jessica's attitude. "The change in how I feel was not a sudden revolution. It happened over the years and it feels like maturation. Now I identify with him. I see that he didn't have a lot of options, that he really had reached a dead end; he was going nowhere and he knew it. His behavior toward me and the way he died make a certain kind of sense. I still feel bad that my life is a lot easier and I have options he never had, but I see that the things I was angry at are things I couldn't understand. What my father did was devastating, but forgivable; he was loving and sincere. Although the suicide was partly an act of aggression toward me, I always felt he really loved me; in a way he didn't abandon me."

Forgiving a beloved father who has betrayed you always entails forgiving yourself for the hatred his betrayal evoked in you. Jessica accomplished both in the middle of her life.

These two daughters, one blue blood and the other blue collar, forgave their fathers at different times for different reasons, but they followed the same basic course. They both started out blaming themselves, then blamed the other, and finally blamed nobody.

T HE scene around Dana Reinhardt's Christmas tree epitomizes holiday joy—her friends, relatives, assorted children and grandchildren, and Dana's second husband Tom are with her. There is also always a present and a place at the table for Dana's first husband Saul, from whom she has been divorced for two decades.

Holidays were far less jolly when the Reinhardts were married. Dana spent many special occasions by herself while Saul slept off a drunken binge or came home late from a "faculty meeting" with one of his retinue of girlfriends at the college where they both taught. Worst of all, he was absent when Dana had to put their teenage son in a drug detoxification program. Fortunately, the boy recovered, Saul eventually sobered up, and Dana divorced him and married a man who loved taking care of her.

"I really have forgiven him because I don't resent him any more," Dana told me. She was a funny, thoughtful woman whose life experience has given her a refreshing candor. "He did a lot of creepy things, but I still see him— he's the father of my children. Once I divorced him he reformed after twenty-five years." She didn't take him back because "I didn't believe the recovery."

Time has changed things for both of them. "Lots of

things happened that were hard to forgive, but the kids grew up and he finally took responsibility. He's a decent person now; he tries very hard. He's an old man, and without drinking he's a good man, but he was always eccentric and now he's very eccentric." Could she have forgiven him if he hadn't reformed? "I don't think so—although if he drank and I wasn't married to him I might just feel sorry for him." How far a person is willing to go toward forgiving is often determined by circumstances. The change in Dana's fortunes has made the pain Saul caused peripheral rather than central—and she frankly admits that the contrast between her success and his failure does not hurt.

Aging has made a difference for her, teaching her to marshal her resources and to use her remaining time well. "Anger takes energy; it's a wasteful thing. When you've lived longer than you know you're going to live you prioritize. It's like being on a sinking ship—you get rid of a lot of stuff you don't need."

Resentment is one thing Dana no longer needs because it has been replaced by fulfillment; for the first time in her life, she has enough. Their children don't have to rely on their father, and neither does she. "I'm happily remarried—that has more to do with forgiveness than anything else. My needs are met, all the needs that Saul never could handle. If you're not needy, you're not angry." Her own satisfaction has bred sympathy, and the wish to alleviate her ex-spouse's unhappy last years.

"He always comes for the holidays—he has no place, just a tiny one-room apartment, and I feel he's entitled to be with the kids and grandchildren. He's deaf now, which is extremely isolating. And the woman he's been with ever since we divorced is a terrible woman and the children hate her," she confides with a laugh at how outrageous it sounds. "And I can cook too—it's perfect!" Living well is not only the best revenge; it is the best forgiveness.

FORGIVING fulfills different needs at the various stages of life. On the cusp of adulthood, Sophia Agnoletti was determined to set her course correctly. Pardoning her father meant growing up in ways he never could, taking charge, and coming into her own. Only in middle age could Jessica Kramer empathize and sympathize with the state of mind that drove her middle-aged father to suicide. Because she needed experience to make her insight real rather than abstract, she could never have identified with his predicament until she reached the same time in life herself. The loving sorrow she was able to feel at fifty would have been impossible earlier, no matter how hard she tried. Her experience shows why exhorting someone to forgive prematurely never works. At seventy, Dana Reinhardt had achieved greater happiness than she ever had before. With healthy perversity, she could take pleasure in how much better off she was than the now-elderly man who had hurt her long ago; the prospect of her coming separation from everything made her separation from victimhood possible. As everyone must, each of them found her own time and season for forgiveness.

5

How We Forgive III:
The Unrepentant
and the Dead

How do you forgive the unrepentant and the dead? One will not, and the other cannot, apologize or make amends for the wrong they have done; dialogue with either is equally impossible except inside your own head. Both force prospective forgivers to rely only on themselves, or to get validation from third parties—a much more indirect and complicated route.

Tragically, the passage of time has no impact on those who feel no remorse; if anything, it calcifies their denial or self-righteousness. This adds an additional layer of disappointment for those who continue to long for a sign of regret, an admission of guilt, or an act of reparation; repeatedly dashing hopes for the apology that never comes is another betrayal. Only when death removes all possibility of reconciliation are they forced to accept that the work of resolution is theirs alone.

Death can open up as many opportunities as it cuts off. When the culprit is removed from the scene—and punished—all further mistreatment comes to an end. The finality of death brings distance and separation that can profoundly alter the victim's perspective and prospects in ways not imaginable while the perpetrator lived; the ultimate limitation may make mourning possible, and without mourning there can be no resolution.

Acts of unrepentant cruelty by the living or the dead are the hardest things to forgive because they provoke the deepest forces of hatred, and self-hatred (the worse you have been treated by someone you love, the more you hate yourself for having loved that person). Resolving any betrayal mobilizes creative energy; these betrayals take the most. Personal achievement, even when not directly related to the trauma, is the best way to get the affirmation the betrayer will never provide. It is a public statement that you are not defined or confined by what someone has done to you.

An incestuous mother, a physically brutal father, and an emotionally destructive lover damaged the lives of three people and never showed remorse. Each victim forgave via a creative endeavor—a film, a book, and a business.

MAGGIE Alexander found a unique way to pardon her mother for committing one of the most fundamental violations a child can endure: she wrote and directed the first documentary film ever made about mother/daughter incest. Maggie's mother sexually molested her and then denied her crime when confronted by her adult daughter with what Rabbi Posner had called "the awful specifics."

Both of Maggie's parents categorically rejected her accusation without asking any questions or showing concern about how she felt. "It was excruciating," she recalled. "All my mother said was 'It couldn't have happened—I didn't even enjoy sex with your father.'" The only response she ever got from her mother afterward was a terse card that said, "Sorry you're in so much pain," and a threatening note from her father: "We won't see you again unless you take back what you said."

Maggie responded by telling her tale to the world in her film *Stories Nobody Wants to Listen To.* "It was art therapy for myself," she said. "As soon as I remembered what happened I had a huge upsurge of creative energy. I'd felt like a freak because this was a kind of incest you never hear about—since it happens between women it's lowest on the hierarchy. I decided to do a film so others would feel less isolated." It was shown in a documentary festival at a museum in her hometown; nobody from her family attended.

The movie, which included autobiographical footage as well as interviews with other victims of maternal incest, was more than a public service; it was a public denunciation of Maggie's mother. Maggie provided a forum for these women to break the secrecy that is one of the most destructive aspects of their ordeal, while simultaneously convicting her own mother without giving her a chance to defend herself; now, the daughter was in control. The audience's reaction punished the mother even as it validated the daughter's sense of reality. Filming an exposé about your own mother's perversion is a far more potent act of vengeance than "dressing to kill" or pushing a coffee cup across a table, but it, too, is a socially appropriate outlet for hostility.

Producing this work of art, with its multiplicity of

motives, altered its creator's state of mind. "There was absolutely no way I could forgive her until I had first let out my rage. I see why people avoid things; I gained fifteen pounds editing that video. I eventually realized that putting all my energy into hating her just tied me to her and depleted me. I've reclaimed myself."

Maggie's course of action was forgiving instead of merely vindictive because she did more than just "let out rage." Expressing hostility must never be an end in itself; it is only a precondition to moving on.

Compassion and insight can be born when outrage dissipates. Committing incest, Maggie saw, had been her mother's bizarre way to get her daughter to nurture her. "I started to pity her. I knew that she despised herself and expected me to be her mother; she had no way not to be what she was." What Maggie once thought was a malevolent act she now recognized as the expression of a damaged will—still terrible, but very human.

Even without her mother's participation, Maggie has managed to retrieve something from their relationship. "I can identify with her now. I used to feel ripped apart when I tried to remember the good things in the context of incest, but I've come to appreciate that I got my artistic talent from her; she was an actress."

Maggie's parents have not reestablished contact with her. "It's still painful that they don't want to see me, even though not going home has been ninety percent relief and only ten percent sorrow. It's made me have to forgive them twice—once for childhood and again for refusing to see me now. I recognize that we have parallel truths which will never intersect, and that neither of us will change. I can live with it and not keep doubting."

Echoing what Sophia Agnoletti said about her playboy father, Maggie said, "I know that I am the stronger one, that I faced it and she couldn't." The film she made and the forgiveness that followed were Maggie's way to convert her powerlessness into strength, symbolically killing and then sparing the mother who will never face the truth. "I slayed the dragon," she concluded with quiet triumph.

Exonerating an unrepentant person is never a purely altruistic act. Doing so induces a justifiable sense of moral superiority and harnesses hostility as creative energy. Behavior need not be seen as self-sacrificing for its benefits— to self and others—to be appreciated.

A situation like Maggie's, the example I posed to Rabbi Posner and Father Neuhaus, epitomizes the divide between Judaism and Christianity over forgiveness. The rabbi would find her forgiveness admirable; the priest would consider it necessary. I believe that when the perpetrator of so grievous an assault shows no remorse, whether to forgive ought to be entirely at the discretion of the person who suffered it. The violated one should strive to attenuate hatred and transcend victimhood because of the personal cost of perpetuating these states of mind, but going further depends on individual needs and resources.

While Maggie derived undeniable gratification from telling her story to a shocked, packed auditorium, validation on a smaller scale can be just as effective. For most people, making a public statement about intimate betrayal is as likely as the fantasy of my patient who wished that her own sexual molestation could be splashed in headlines across the front page of the *New York Times*. Private sympathy and outrage on one's behalf by loved ones may be all a person can elicit, but it suffices.

GROWING up and no longer living at home separated Maggie from her abusive mother; Christopher Young's father and David Darielle's lover had to die before the cruelty they inflicted ceased. Only then could Christopher and David begin to prosper and to forgive their tormentors. This is typical for victims of tyranny.

Christopher Young's father's friends put glowing tributes in the newspaper when this scholarly, cultured man died. Christopher, however, knew a more ominous side of his father's character. "He was gentle with everyone but me, and everyone loved him but me," said the dark-eyed thirty-four-year-old biblical scholar. From earliest childhood, Mr. Young had mocked and beaten Christopher, trying to crush his spirit when he disagreed in any way with his father's wishes. Once at a family party, fearing that his seven-year-old son would become homosexual, Mr. Young—who, as Christopher later learned, was himself bisexual—hit him for dancing with unseemly abandon. "The most horrible thing was that whenever we argued he'd go to bed with heart problems. The doctor would come and I'd start crying over him. Then when he finally died the doctor said that his heart had been so strong." It infuriated Christopher that his father had used even his son's concern to manipulate and control him. As a result, Christopher recapitulated their sado-masochistic bond in homosexual encounters with dangerous strangers.

Mr. Young's attempt at a final apology had been characteristic. "On his deathbed he tried to touch me with his foot, and said 'I don't know if I should have loved you

more or punished you more.' I thought it was too late—
he had done things against me all his life and then asks
me this. I didn't want to hold his hand but I did; it felt
ridiculous but there was also something good about it; he
did make that gesture." This touch, ambivalent though it
was, was the precursor to forgiveness.

A son can be relieved and liberated by the death of
such a father, and few have changed their lives as dramatically as a result. "Immediately afterward, I went abroad
to study archeology, which is what I really loved. I
learned five languages, and got three degrees in three
years. My relationship with my mother improved signifi-
cantly. I also fell in love with a woman for the first time.
She accepts me just as I am, and we married recently. I
had been dependent on my father financially and emotionally, and what I did was defined by his views. Now
that he's gone I don't have to ask anyone's permission. I
feel more confident than I ever did before; the things I've
achieved since his death showed me that I'm not the despicable person he thought I was."

Recognizing his own worth, and accomplishing so
much so quickly, had another, unexpected effect on Christopher; he found himself thinking that his father was not
as despicable as he had believed. "Strangely enough, I
can sympathize with him now. He was probably very unhappy—he must have seen himself in me and hated and
punished himself through me." Christopher has also realized that he has elements of his father's character. "I share
his orderliness, and I get angry the same way he did." The
separation imposed by death created a boundary between
Christopher and his father that permitted him to see the
truth about both of them. He no longer repudiates the

part of himself that is like his father because he no longer hates either his father or himself. Converting hatred to anger as he did is the most important step anyone can take in coming to terms with betrayal.

Christopher charted how his feelings had shifted. "It started as fear, then anger, then indifference, and now I feel positive indifference. There's still a lot of anger underneath, but I'm more lenient with him—I can sympathize. I can't say I forgive him but I do say 'poor man.' "

Despite Christopher's disclaimer, "positive indifference" qualifies as forgiveness. His hatred has dissipated, he has reclaimed positive aspects of the relationship, and he has found something in his father's character with which to identify. Ambiguous states and partial resolutions like his are more common than we think. People often have the mistaken notion—endorsed by much of the literature on forgiveness and even by the dictionary—that genuine forgiveness must be uncontaminated by any negative emotion, to be genuine and transformative. The extraordinary changes in Christopher's life that followed from his new attitude toward his father demonstrate that anger need not vanish for forgiveness to be real; it need only cease to prevail. If a posthumous relationship is better than the living one was, forgiveness has occurred.

Christopher left out the most significant thing father and son share. Until we spoke, he never realized that his revised view of his father dated from the recent publication of his own first book, the only modern translation of a mystical text of the biblical period. Thus, without knowing it, he perpetuated his father's scholarship, but in a field of his own choosing. It was an achievement that, he knew, would have made his father proud.

Christopher's rebirth after his father's death not only celebrated his new freedom, but also showed his victorious pleasure at being alive when his tormentor was not. Hostile triumph of this kind is a buried, but virtually universal, aspect of forgiving the dead, which traditionalists condemn and which many people feel horrified and guilty to discover within themselves. It fulfills the healthy function of liberating a person from an oppressive relationship.

The death of his father inspired Christopher to develop his talent and discover his own identity. Losing a viciously deprecating lover to AIDs had the same effect on David Darielle.

Thirty-seven-year-old David is the consummate host in his cozy, quirky little French restaurant. We talked over a glass of wine at his perch by the front door of the café, which embodies his personal style—mismatched chairs, shabbily chic slipcovered couches by the fireplace, masses of flowers everywhere. David greeted most diners by name, exchanging gossip and Continental-style embraces. He got up periodically to chat with his guests and keep an eye of the staff—a man comfortably in charge of his domain.

Two years earlier, I had visited David in the barren little room of the locked mental ward where he sat despondent. He had checked himself in for the weekend after hurling a heavy flower pot at his skeletal, hateful, dying lover Allen, whom he could easily have killed if his aim had been better. Allen died shortly afterward, refusing David's abject apologies and frantic attempts to make amends, leaving a legacy of rage, guilt, and bitterness that David has only recently put aside.

Allen had been David's partner in life and business for six years when AIDs struck him. Cool and remote, he had little in common with the emotional, gregarious David beyond the esthetic sense they shared and the restaurant they created together, its name an amalgam of theirs. Their relationship, always tumultuous and tinged with cruelty, turned vicious as Allen's illness progressed. "People can blame it on dementia," said David, "but I believe his personality was never a loving one. It was a kind of self-punishment for me to be there. He controlled everything and kept repeating that I wasn't interesting or talented. I felt I had to stay and take it because it was 'the right thing to do.' I said to myself, 'He has a death sentence and I can't make it any worse for him.' After I threw the plant he never talked to me again, although he continued to accept my help. He wasn't a forgiving person—he wouldn't talk to his own mother when she called the hospital. He couldn't forgive himself."

A combination of survivor's guilt, compassion, and a history of desperately trying to please unpleasant people compelled David to sacrifice himself. For three harrowing years, he followed Allen's commands and endured his insults, receiving in return not a word of tenderness or gratitude, until the man he devotedly nursed abandoned him utterly and died all alone.

David's initial reaction to Allen's death was to retreat into cynicism and despair. He was barely able to keep himself and his business functioning. "The most destructive part of his illness was that it made me numb for years—I didn't let myself feel anything. It was like a vacuum. I turned the anger I couldn't direct at him on my employees; I fought with everybody. Allen thrived on anger, but I didn't."

The time came when David realized the toll that nursing his grudge was taking. "I couldn't go on forever with only resentment, anger, and frustration, not allowing anyone to get close to me." Like most of us, David changed only when he could not bear staying the same any longer.

A conversation changed his life. Many forgivers say that talking was their royal road to resolution, and that the sound of their own voice—especially directed at a sympathetic listener—helped them more than anything else. David explained, "My thought process works best through talking as a form of resolving—I'm a real blabbermouth. One day I said to a dear friend, 'I'm carrying Allen's curse, I can't date a decent person.' Then I saw it's not really a curse—I'm just not ready to let anybody into my life because of what I've gone through. The curse was nine years with him, a relationship based on fear of AIDs, disillusionment with the dating practices of gay men in the 1980s, and the difficulty of meeting somebody I could fall in love with. I couldn't blame him forever, blame him for everything; everything isn't his fault. It's so easy to have a scapegoat, but I was also to blame because I was with him. What I am today was part of what I was in my past. I was trapped because I was not developed enough and too fearful, and I had grown up learning not to hurt anybody."

With his insight, David wrested control of his life from Allen's ghost. Forgiving began when he ceased defining himself as the passive victim of another's cruelty. Only then does the energy bound up in hating an injurious person become available for living and loving.

It was essential that David recognize how he co-created his bondage to Allen. There is always some element of participation, if only at the level of emotional engagement, even between an abusive parent and a dependent child, and certainly between two adults. Acknowledging your active involvement in any relationship, based on your needs and your history, means that a trauma did not simply befall you, and that its impact can therefore be modified by your own efforts. I had the same critical recognition myself.

Understanding his own motivation revived David's entrepreneurial spirit, and his business blossomed. He is negotiating with his landlord to buy the entire building of which he now rents the ground floor so that he can expand the restaurant, a risk Allen would surely have vetoed. He has also made up with staff and customers he alienated when Allen was dying. "People I'd fought with came back to have dinner just last week," he told me. "It brought me to tears"— tears of grief for what he had done and suffered and relief that it was over.

David has also sold the isolated country cabin that Allen had pressured him to buy, and purchased another, far more welcoming, retreat. "The new house is all mine; it was a symbolic step to buy it."

In the interest of retaining anything he can that was good, David has been careful not to discard everything of Allen's. In a loving act of remembrance, despite everything, he has placed a framed photograph of Allen amid the candelabra and flowers on the mantelpiece of the restaurant's fireplace, and retained its original name. He has made their joint enterprise his own, but, with a mixture of recognition and regret, gives his partner the credit he is due. "If not for him I would never be in this business. I learned a lot from him, even though it would have been much easier to take a class." Most important, David sees what he himself had contributed all along: "I was more central to our success than I ever realized. Last night was superb—I did a splendid party, and I was so proud of what I've created. Now I'm taking credit when somebody says 'the place is so beautiful, did you design it?' I say, 'I did.'"

Some people have to die before they can be forgiven. "After death you can forgive without confronting the person because you're not putting anybody at fault; you're only dealing with yourself. You don't have to blame anybody or anything—it's easier." When he could no longer do either, David finally stopped trying to please or to avoid hurting Allen. He abandoned his hope that their relationship could change. "When things happen I still want to tell him, but I can imagine what the conversation would be. I understand now that that is the way he was made; it couldn't ever be different."

David handed me his new business card as I left. Under the name of the restaurant, it now reads, "David Darielle, Proprietor."

A former patient of mine was a gifted ballerina. She never joined a major dance company because every time she had an important audition, she felt compelled to leave town to take care of her mother, who was always, it seemed, conveniently on the verge of a mental breakdown. My patient used to pace her apartment haranguing her nemesis in absentia, muttering, "You ruined my life and destroyed my career" even after her mother had been dead for thirty years. How did Maggie, Christopher, and David avoid a similar fate? All three were ambitious and persistent. They forced themselves to face reality and made efforts to understand, and even to sympathize with, those who had harmed them. Their creative projects, which they, unlike my patient, saw to completion, helped them establish independent identities and provided external validation of their own value and viewpoints. Through their work, they preserved something of value from their relationships to significant figures in their lives and also became less dependent on them. A combination of luck, talent, and character provided them with the resources to modify the malignant influence, now carried within, of their betrayers. They did not escape unscathed—their personal and professional lives bear scars of tragedy—but they escaped.

An element of sadistic triumph is a necessary component of forgiving the unrepentant and the dead. Maggie achieved this by publicly humiliating her betrayer on film; Christopher and David by outliving theirs. Hostility humanely discharged through art—whether in living or in a creative project—is the forgiver's secret weapon.

6

Reconciliation

I never fully understood what a reconciliation feels like until I presided over one. A patient of mine had been estranged from her father for years, with good reason; he had turned her into a prostitute for his private pleasure. He contacted me when he learned from her brother that she had become a drug addict and had gone into therapy at age thirty-five.

It was disconcerting to hear what sounded like genuine concern in the voice of the man I had come to hate as much as his daughter did—a brilliant and successful scientist who had perverted his ingenuity into devising methods of spying on his prepubescent child while she was undressing and later paid her handsomely to take her blouse off for him ("When I became aroused as he was looking at me I thought I didn't deserve to live any more," she had told me.) With her consent, after seeing him and establishing that his angst was real, I arranged for them to meet in my office.

The scene was every wronged person's fantasy of retribution. He listened to every accusation, acknowledged them all, wept with guilt and remorse. He told her he had always loved her, reminded her of evidence to prove it, and vowed to make amends.

I was unprepared for his daughter's reaction, and my own. Instead of triumphant outrage, or even pleasure at his agony and despair, we both felt sorrow and pain on his behalf. He seemed not evil, but pitiable, weak, and broken by the knowledge that he had crippled the person who meant the most to him. There was even a moment of black humor: At one point, after he insisted that his happiest hours had been spent with her when she was growing up, she said only half ironically, "Then why didn't you just take me bowling?" The tragic insights of their reconciliation affected the observer as much as the participants.

Though their subsequent relationship has been rocky, fraught with recriminations and manipulations on her part, and irritated defensiveness on his, the meeting transformed both their lives. The father subsequently met and married a woman who knew the story and pardoned him. The daughter entered a drug rehabilitation program and stuck with it for the first time in numerous attempts. She has now been drug-free and much more stable for fifteen years. There is no doubt that she recovered her will to live by witnessing her father's contrition and accepting his apology.

To be reunited with the one who has betrayed your trust, to hear a heartfelt confession and embrace again, is the longed-for culmination of forgiveness. This ideal reflects the fundamental human desire for attachment, vindication, and catharsis—for evidence that at least sometimes virtue is rewarded and people see the light.

Both Jews and Christians consider reconciliation the supreme goal, the model for conduct, and the metaphor for God's relationship to sinful humanity. This theme has a powerful hold on the imagination and has been the subject of great drama since before the Prodigal Son came home. A film critic told me he thinks such scenes are so popular in movies precisely because they are so rare in real life.

In the moment of reconciliation, years of pain can seem to melt away. While the memory of the damage never can—and probably never should—be erased, love reestablished can be even more poignant and precious than a bond that was never severed; the new relationship is more real, based as it now is on mutual recognition and awareness of frailty.

Everytime someone described a reconciliation to me, I found myself close to tears; I was never able to have this with my father while he lived, and I envied it.

Reconciliation takes three forms. The first is mutual rapprochement, as Henry Mann and his ill father experienced in the hospital. In the second type, the one who is at fault approaches the victim, admits guilt, and asks pardon. The injured party reaches out to the perpetrator unprompted in the third, the most atypical and remarkable variety. This is the Christian paradigm, and I only saw one instance of it, by a Jewish agnostic. Tammy Kaye—the same redheaded dancer who pushed her coffee cup across the table toward her unfaithful lover as a young woman, in middle age made up with the mother she had always hated.

Tammy's mother had never wanted children, but acceded to the wishes of her husband, who doted on his little daughter. "She hated me as a rival before I came out of the womb, and he took total possession of me from the moment I was born," Tammy recounted. "He spoiled me rotten and I had no relationship with her." The man who was "the center of the universe" for both mother and daughter suddenly died at the age of forty-two, leaving Tammy "in an alien world" with a mother who blamed her husband's premature death on his working too hard so he could lavish his daughter with presents. "Then she and I went to war, and from the time I was twelve years old I despised, vilified, and rejected her rejection of me." Home life was so unbearable that Tammy left at seventeen and rarely saw or spoke to her tormentor again until she herself turned forty—the age her mother was when Mr. Kaye died.

Tammy had an "epiphany" on her fortieth birthday. Her corrosive hatred was the one thing in her life she felt she had no control over. "My relationship with my mother was the worst wound I had, and I decided to try to change it, whatever it took. That was my project for myself, and I was perfectly willing to fail."

Step one in her project was seeing things through her mother's eyes. "I began to say, 'It must have been really shitty in 1951—there were no single mothers then.' She had to run a business, manage her own life, and she knew how to do nothing but cook and she didn't like that. I suddenly realized this and considered the possibility that she was not malintentioned, not truly evil. With all my understanding I had never before imagined that her behavior could be anything but malevolent."

To deepen her awareness, Tammy sought professional assistance. "I went to a therapist to work on this specific issue. He said one thing that changed my life: 'See yourself going to the refrigerator. You're starving—you can't wait to get there—but when you do you find it totally empty. See your refrigerator and understand that your mother is emotionally bankrupt, not intentionally destructive—not someone who didn't want to love you, but someone incapable of loving.' I finally got it. His words have never left me."

Cold, ungiving people always accuse those who need them of being voracious. The metaphor showed Tammy that her emotional hunger had not caused the "refrigerator's" emptiness. In addition, it showed her that she did not deserve her mother's hatred; as long as she thought she was the daughter of a monster, she secretly felt monstrous herself. Realizing that her mother was damaged rather than demonic vindicated Tammy, made Tammy pity her mother, and paved the way for love.

The next phase of Tammy's transformation happened a decade later on her fiftieth birthday, and it came upon her unbidden. She was hosting a lavish party for herself with one hundred friends when Mrs. Kaye called, as self-involved as ever. "There I was surrounded by the most important people in my life, at this event which I'd created for them to share with me—something totally generous—and she started talking about herself and someone she knew who had just died. I thanked her for wishing me happy birthday, hung up the phone, and started to weep. That was the moment of letting go. I didn't need to hate her ever again, and I felt serene."

Tammy's weeping signaled the beginning of her ability to mourn, without which forgiveness never happens. It expressed her sense of loss, her pity for her mother's emotional bankruptcy, her recognition that she had always longed for the love her mother had withheld. Her tears showed that her defensive "rejection of [her mother's] rejection" was breaking down, and with it her need to be as cold and abandoning to her mother as her mother had been toward her. Grieving dissolved her need to retaliate.

In the following year, Tammy changed course. Eschewing the freelance life, she became a businesswoman and opened a dance studio. And she decided to go home for the first time in years. As is so often the case in reconciliations between adult children and their aging parents, the proximate cause of her visit was a medical problem of her mother's. "She was going to have surgery, and I wanted her to know she was safe. I decided it was the right thing to do, even though she had never been there for me during my six operations. I became the mommy in a calculated way, and created a relationship with her where I'm the kind of mother I wanted her to be."

Then Tammy did something extraordinary. As she had years earlier in her dramatic restaurant scene, she once again called on her acting skills at a critical moment. "I told my mother I loved her. I didn't really, but I told her because I knew she needed it. Doing this was loving the empty refrigerator and accepting it with its limitations."

Her mother's response was just as extraordinary: "In giving her love I didn't truly feel she became this little bubby with all this love waiting inside her. My saying that created something that had never been there; it was like unzipping it." This reaction turned Tammy's faked love into the real thing, and mother and daughter connected for the first time. "Since then I've had a completely new and different relationship with her. This year she's had two strokes and a heart attack, and I've gone to take care of her. I've given deep abiding love that now is genuine. I see she's evolved and I never believed it was possible. My forgiveness of her has created the possibility of her giving love back. I never held out any hope for her; now we speak almost every day. We're reconciled on almost everything. It's a phenomenal metamorphosis. People can change until the day they die."

Tammy's definition of forgiveness transcends the dictionary's "cessation of resentment" into realms that Father Neuhaus would approve. "It's not just accepting the limits. It's loving the person not despite but *for* those things— with those things and because of them." Now Tammy fervently believes that her mother's own emotional hunger, masked for forty years, deserves her daughter's compassion. "I have unconditional love, which she now also feels for me. I wanted it for so long from her. My giving her love and articulating it to and for her freed her to express something she might otherwise not have experienced in her life. It's amazing to have a rich relationship with her."

Tammy's mother recently turned eighty-five, and they celebrated together. "I gave her a party in the hospital. She said 'I feel like I've discovered you. I never appreciated you.' Her time was almost up; I've helped her have a life again. I know many of my contemporaries will die hating their parents. They never resolve it and they'll have an unhealed wound. I was on a path to take this curse to her grave and mine. Something happened and I had the opportunity to change that. I feel so blessed." What would have happened if her mother hadn't responded to her efforts? "I couldn't have gone so far. I would have had to keep my distance," Tammy admitted. Reconciliation, unlike forgiveness, always takes two.

What was the "something" that permitted Tammy to take the riskiest and most rewarding step of her life? "My family never forgives and never forgets. I would have been perfectly capable of that too; I'm breaking the mold." Forgiving her mother was a way to construct an identity distinct from her family. Without conscious intention or awareness, the person she chose to emulate instead was Jesus Christ; loving her enemy made her enemy love her back.

Although it is not possible, or necessary, to fully explain an inspired gratuitous act, several emotional factors shaped Tammy's decision to behave as she did. The desire to be different from her family, and more specifically, from her mother in her "refrigerator" days, was paramount. Timing also played a role; Tammy could empathize with a overwhelmed middle-aged widow when she herself turned forty, just as Jessica Kramer grasped her suicidal father's predicament when she reached the age he was when his life fell apart. Being in a position superior both financially and emotionally to her mother's at the same age made Tammy feel victorious as well as generous. Then, at fifty, she grieved for her lost possibilities surrounded by friends at a banquet she had provided; she could embrace the old empty refrigerator now that her own was overflowing with good things. As Dana Reinhardt said when she explained forgiving her ex-husband late in life, "when you're less needy, you're less angry."

Tammy had to conquer her hatred because it made her feel like her mother. Tammy's actions proved to her that she was not a refrigerator herself; she had something to give. Extending kindness to her mother atoned for her hatred; her mother's respose made her feel powerful, lovable, and good. Since Mrs. Kaye rose to the occasion, Tammy's bold strategy enriched both their lives. Together they created mutual consolation for the time they had missed and the little time they had left, a testimony to love, will, and human possibility.

Just as death permitted Christopher Young and David Darielle to pardon betrayals they never could have during the perpetrators' lifetimes, it galvanized a wrongdoer to ask for pardon. For Calvin Westfield's father, the fatal illness of one son caused him to reassess, regret, and make restitution for how he had treated his other one. At the end of his own life, Mr. Westfield was able to correct his conduct and improve his character. But he couldn't have done it without his son Calvin's loving response.

Calvin had always been baffled and devastated by the blatant favoritism his father, a wealthy and formidable entrepreneur, showed toward Calvin's older brother. Although Calvin was the one who most admired and resembled him both physically and intellectually, the authoritarian Mr. Westfield oppressed, undermined, and belligerently belittled the boy throughout his youth. Like Christopher Young's father, he tried to crush his son's will. "Nothing was ever my own. My father had a withering glance, and you sensed his coldness if everything wasn't exactly the way he wanted it. He was frightening and powerful."

Mr. Westfield's final act of rejection was to disinherit Calvin and make his brother a multimillionaire by his fortieth birthday. Calvin discovered this by accident; his father never even informed him that he had done so. In self-protection, Calvin withdrew from his family, and took up a profession outside the family business. He struggled constantly with his feelings of depression and abandonment. "His cruelty tore me to pieces, and I cracked under the strain. I felt like a body with a hollow voice, or no voice at all. The pain was so searing that it remains to this day."

A grim accident of fate provided an opportunity for change. Had Calvin's brother not developed a malignant brain tumor that proved fatal after several terrible years, father and son might well have remained permanently estranged. Fortunately for them both, the loss of his older son shocked the father into realizing that he had alienated and mistreated the child he had left. Grief and remorse fueled his resolve to make amends.

The change was subtle, but cumulative. "There was never a major breakthrough, but I think he saw what a disappointment he had been as my father, and he became friendlier. I started speaking to him, and gradually he figured out I had a positive attitude. He grew more positive and less nasty. Eventually he said, 'I never realized how intelligent you were, how nice you were.' It felt like he was finally getting to know me." In words virtually identical to the ones Tammy's mother used, Calvin's father discovered he had a son who had been worthy of his love and admiration all along. By mourning for his own failings as a parent, he finally became a good one.

Calvin's attitude completed the reconciliation. Like Tammy, he had always longed to be close to his father and was able to put aside his wounded fury when given the opportunity. "I reached a point in life where I could take him literally—that's my forgiveness. If my father only discovered something worthy about me at age seventy-five that he never noticed or wanted to see before, I accept that he just saw it. I take no offense now. I'm pleased he found it out at all and he could compliment me and think about it. Having your father think about you defines a son and his worth, at least in childhood. It makes life now much more meaningful to have a father who suddenly— even if it's just suddenly—woke up and recognized me."

A reconciliation late in life is always bittersweet because of all the time that can never be recaptured. Calvin's father is now eighty-six and dying himself from a heart condition. "He hasn't got long to live. He'll miss me and I'll miss him and we'll miss the good feeling we've finally created over these past few years. We refer to it as our 'mutual admiration society'—we don't ask the other to be what he's not. I wish we could have more time; we've had too little as father and son."

What bothers Calvin the most is that Mr. Westfield cannot travel to admire the commercial property that Calvin negotiated for on his own and is in the process of renovating. "Though we speak every day about it as long as his endurance holds up, we both know he'll never see it. He gets excited and wants to live when we talk about it; he's proud that I did something he didn't do. He told me, 'I wouldn't have had the patience—you recognized the value. I couldn't have taken such a risk.' He's very impressed with my achievement. We also talk about the past, what a good father I am, how I really think about my children and understand them. He wishes he could have been better but he didn't know how. Now I bear him no ill will; I actually love him unconditionally."

Calvin too now knows that his father was limited, not wicked. "One day he said, 'I don't know why I treated you the way I did. The only thing I can think of is I was competitive with you.' 'How could you compete with a small child?' I asked. He honestly doesn't know." Competitive no longer, Calvin's personal and professional success are the joy and recompense of his father's old age. "In the end," Calvin concluded, "my father and I ended up with a good relationship. What more could either of us ask for?"

What Calvin's father asked for, and his son was able to grant him, was a second chance.

WHETHER it leads to Calvin Westfield's "unconditional love," Christopher Young's "positive indifference," or something in between, every act of forgiving proceeds through three stages: reengagement, recognition, and reinterpretation. Reengagement is the willingness to relive the betrayal and to reconsider your relationship with the perpetrator. The forgiver then recognizes all the original buried emotions the betrayal elicited—including shame, helplessness, rage, and the desire to retaliate—and acknowledges that what happened cannot be undone, that the experience of loss will forever be part of life even though its meaning can change. This step frees the forgiver from pursuing revenge or denying the impact of the betrayal. Reinterpreting the meaning of the betrayal and recasting the perpetrator's motivation then gives the forgiver a new perspective on the experience. What was passively suffered can then be seen as having been actively created by both parties. For the first time, the forgiver can feel empathy toward, or at least understanding of, the betrayer. From blaming the other and subtly blaming yourself you progress to blaming nobody but holding both the other and yourself accountable.

Forgiving always has willed as well as unwilled components. Both intentional and implicit forgivers have to decide to confront the past and do the work of creating a mental state receptive to increased understanding. However, personal context must be taken into account; creating the environment in which forgiveness could occur is no guarantee that it will.

No one escapes intimate betrayal or the struggle to resolve it. Coming to terms with the deepest traumas of our lives can take a multitude of forms, and can lead to an array of good outcomes. If we are honest and fearless enough, we are rewarded for our efforts with insight, some measure of peace, and when the conditions are right, recovered love.

7

Forgiving Yourself

J ACK O'Reilly didn't fit my image of a cold-blooded killer. This mammoth, jocular man graciously ushered me into a chair in the office of the single-room-occupancy hotel where he lived and kept up a line of engaging, salty patter throughout our interview.

He had been out of the "max joint" (the maximum security penitentiary) for four years, after serving a sentence for conspiracy to commit murder, the most recent felony in his long criminal record. A former member of the Westies, the New York Irish mob so violent that the Mafia farms out their most vicious crimes to them, Jack had been one of their busiest enforcers—"I'm sort of the negotiator," he explained—for twenty-two of his forty-eight years. The job suited him; on closer inspection, I could see that beneath his cordial facade, this glib, six-foot four-inch, three-hundred-pound behemoth was capable of brutality I could barely imagine.

The day he was released from jail, Jack decided to

"start all over and make a new life." He'd left "the family" several times before but, he said, "Once you're with the element they want you." So this son of several generations of policemen would always return because "life on the other side tasted good." "I could have gone back again," he told me. "I could have gotten a luxury apartment, a driver, and a percentage, but when they put the gun on the table I said 'I'm not taking it.' " Having done his time and not ratted on anybody had won him the right to walk away. Despite many temptations and near misses, so far Jack has made good on his pledge. Forswearing the seductive offers, he got a place to live through a social agency instead and landed his first legitimate job as a delivery driver for a chain of discount stores, where he has now been promoted to dispatcher.

He owes it all to a man with a mirror.

In prison, Jack's proportions and his notoriety caused the other inmates to give him a wide berth, and, seething with rage, he used to take his daily walks in the yard alone and undisturbed. One day, a sixty-five-year-old fellow prisoner who was doing consecutive life sentences for five murders joined him. "Who put you here?" his companion asked. Jack recited his usual litany—how the woman who had hired him to kill her husband had framed him and videotaped their transaction in order to get a lighter sentence for her drug-dealing boyfriend. "But who's the problem?" the old man persisted. Jack told him how he'd been the black sheep of his family, how his fiancée had walked out on him, how his father knew he was a thug and ostracized him for years but kissed him goodbye from his death bed. Then his interlocutor took out a mirror, held it up to Jack's face, and said, *"That's* who put you here, that's who the problem is—and that's the one you have to forgive."

"He understood me; he was like my mentor," Jack said in a voice now cleansed of bravado. "He knew he was never getting out, so he became a counselor. He saw that I kept myself separate and I had a chip on my shoulder. 'I know you—you strike terror in everybody, but you're really a gentle guy,' he told me. 'Look in the mirror every time you think somebody hurt you, look in the mirror and see whose problem it is.'" I asked Jack what he had seen in the mirror. "I saw a person who's lonely, stupid, dumb, and a jerk, who could have had everything if I hadn't gone the other way. Most guys in jail say someone else put them there—the cop, their sister—but I tell myself I put myself here because I did the crime and I didn't admit it. I broke that image in jail." I thought of my dream about being an accessory to a murder when he told me this; I too had had to face my responsibility, for a psychological death.

Now, when Jack looks in the mirror, he sees something besides the reflection of his former self. "We had our idols and our big boys in there, but the old man was the top; he was my guiding light. When he died I didn't really lose him—the spiritual was still ingrained in me. I remember what he told me. Every time I want to go back to the element, I close my eyes. I think of him; I promised him. Every day he looks back at me and says, 'Live today.' Then something happens and I don't go back to the boys."

"Here's where your book comes in," he said, displaying the talent that must have served him well in his negotiating days. "I also have to forgive other people, like my family who never came to see me, because I'm the one that did it, not them. People can't say it's the other person, they gotta say it's themselves, that you must have done something that hurt them. You've gotta assume the criticism. For years I'd break your face when somebody said you did something to me; now I listen. I don't want to live like that. That's where I stand. I do more in the city now than I did in my entire life—I go to see the tree in Rockefeller Center, I talk to kids at work about their lives. I forgive because I have to forgive. I look in the mirror every day." With a dose of practicality he added "And besides, the food's terrible in jail."

As I hurried away from him to get back to my own world, I realized that Jack and I had had the same experience, and had come to the same conclusion. The only difference was that someone else had held up the mirror for him, while I had looked into it by myself. Every act of self-forgiveness begins with looking in the mirror and facing what you see there.

Forgiving yourself is the only essential act of forgiveness, because it involves coming to terms with the one person you can never get away from; you can cut off your mother, reject your lover, or repudiate your friend, but there is no escaping yourself for the rest of your life. As Jack and I both discovered, the image of the ultimate culprit stares back at you in your reflection every day, and you ignore it at your peril.

Self-forgiveness, like all genuine forgiveness, begins with the admission of guilt and the proper assignment of fault—in this instance, to oneself—for harm to self and to others. Self-destructive acts rarely spare those we love and are not intended to.

In addition to the three-step resolution process common to all acts of forgiveness, three tasks are specific to self-forgiveness: taking responsibility, grieving for losses you have caused, and hating yourself less as a result. It is the process of forgiving another applied reflexively, a central component of self-acceptance, and the only type of forgiveness that everyone should try to achieve. All effective psychotherapy results in it.

Any act of fully realized forgiveness must include self-forgiveness, because every betrayal provokes vengefulness and hatred in the betrayed, and everybody feels secretly guilty for harboring these unacceptable emotions. People sometimes forgive themselves and the other simultaneously, and sometimes consequentially. In my case, there was an ongoing reciprocity between forgiving my father and forgiving myself. Those who cannot forgive themselves pay a terrible price; inability to do so makes it impossible to forgive anybody else.

TWENTY-SEVEN-YEAR-OLD stockbroker Bruce Peterson used the same word to describe himself in his drinking days that Jack O'Reilly had: "jerk." Since adolescence, he had been obnoxious, arrogant, and belligerent. He threw up on sidewalks, cheated on his girlfriend, and harassed her when she left him. No dramatic intervention, no mentor, therapist, or friend—not even a twelve-step program—persuaded Bruce to change course; he simply got sick of the wreck he was making of his life and slowly, painstakingly, set about transforming it.

First, of course, he had to stop drinking. But, as often happens, sobriety was only the beginning of the solution. "I was dry three months before I realized what I had to forgive myself for," he said. "The way I'd acted revolted me and made me sad for the longest time."

Self-loathing and despair led Bruce to apologize to the woman he had misused. "I was afraid she'd run away in horror, but she was happy that I was sober. I'm lucky I got to see her reaction, and that she wished me well; it meant I didn't need to be forgiven as much as I thought I did." Her acceptance broke the cycle of self-hatred, projection, blaming, and mistreating others that had ruled his life.

Since genuine repentance requires changes in behavior, not merely vows to make them, Bruce decided to begin no relationship until he met a woman he could deeply love. "I started to know real peace only when I acted in ways I believe in."

Bruce identified the same essence of self-forgiveness that Jack O'Reilly and I had discovered. "The biggest thing is admitting my part, seeing that I always participate somehow. This is telling myself the truth." Previously, Bruce had blamed his parents; "I had plenty of ammo, of course," he added.

Forgiveness, like charity, begins at home and becomes a way of life. "Willpower is not really like it is in the movies, where somebody sets his jaw and never strays again; it's more a process of getting worn down by behaving the right way—and not killing myself when I fail. What I used to think of as humility was really self-punishment. I also realize that I hold a grudge when I'm trying to make the other person feel what I feel. This may be superstitious, but I don't want to take too much credit for my progress. I'm just catching up in maturity to everybody else, and so I'm only quietly triumphant."

A jolt of recognition can change the course of a life. Witnessing a gratuitous act of violence galvanized Dan Snyder, a homeless gang member, to find employment, pardon himself, and then to reconcile with his mother, who had turned him out of the house when he was an adolescent. A twenty-six-year-old machinist who is studying to become an evangelical minister, Dan took time out from writing his first sermon to discuss his life with me.

Dan lived on the streets for three years after his mother threw him out. He drank, "dated wild women," dodged the police, and spent most nights sleeping on a bench in downtown Cleveland. There he saw the incident that gave him a foretaste of his destiny. "I remember a man standing on the corner. The leader of my gang had just had a fight with his girlfriend, and for no reason he hit this man and knocked him out; it was just one punch. The guy was innocent, and he had no right to hit him. I looked at that and said 'My God, is this what I'm becoming? I can't be like him; I can't bring myself to do that.' Something turned on inside me and I said, 'Dan, you don't want to be known as scum; you want to have a family.' So I got a job and stuck with it. I lost it, but I got another." Dan, too, mentioned the central role of assuming personal responsibility in his current life. "I'm not a rebel like I used to be. When people criticized me I used to take it as an act against me, but I started taking it like a man."

Part of Dan's new definition of manliness was to forgive his mother, a decision he made intuitively even before his religious conversion. "On my twenty-first birthday, instead of celebrating by drinking, I decided to call my mother. I said, 'I want to dedicate my birthday to you because you carried me for nine months, and I want to thank you for how you acted because it turned my life around. I take responsibility for what I've done and I want to make you proud.' She was dumbfounded— she started to cry, apologized, said she didn't mean to kick me out, and if she had it to do over she'd never have done it. I thanked her for making me go through it; if she'd kept me with her I might never have changed. I thought I should forgive her because it was the right thing to do; I have to be accountable."

When he makes his debut in the pulpit, his mother will be sitting in the front row.

Two women I know had to ask forgiveness of their own bodies for two different types of misuse—one a former prostitute, the other an anorectic who narrowly escaped starving herself to death. Such retrospective acts of self-forgiveness are the culmination of long years of effort, self-examination, and mourning.

I recalled that my friend Nancy Sheridan, a petite advertising executive whose gentle manner belies enormous drive and determination, had battled an eating disorder when she was a graduate student, but I had not been aware that she had documented her ordeal in a series of photographs and was touched that she offered to show them to me. The first couple of snapshots were sweet and funny—Nancy as a girl posing next to her mother who looked more like her older sister, then Nancy as a teenage flower child, with her long straight hair; ethnic-inspired shift; and open, innocent face. I was not prepared for the third: Nancy as a naked, seventy-nine-pound skeleton, with a doomed, vacant expression, waiting to die. "I took

these to record what was happening to me, to try desperately to give myself some perspective," she told me. She
only faced the reality that she was killing herself when
she got off a plane to go to a conference and her own
brother did not recognize her.

Self-forgiveness is the final and continuing stage of a
curative process that has involved years of therapy, meditation, and sorrow over what Nancy did to herself. She
had been an outstanding graduate student in sociology,
publishing twelve articles while writing her dissertation.
"I was programmed for stardom, and being groomed for
a top job in my field," she said. "I tried to please everybody, and I felt so emotionally fragile that the only thing
I could control was food." The tension became intolerable
when her husband was offered a university post in one
part of the country, and her adviser was pressing her to
apply for another hundreds of miles in the opposite direction. Stopping eating was the only way Nancy knew to
protest an untenable situation without directly disappointing anybody. "I got sick, and let sickness be my way to
choose not to comply. I was speaking a body language
that took me off the hook, but at terrible cost."

Soon after her brother's horrified reaction to her spec-
tral appearance, Nancy too looked in the mirror. "I saw
my own reflection one day and it was just a skull—it
frightened me. I also looked down at my plate at lunch
and saw I had taken just three scallops and had scraped
the breading off; this wasn't enough food to survive. To
realize that I had only been pretending to nourish myself
wasn't yet forgiveness; it was just the will to live."

The sequence of events that ultimately led Nancy to
forgive herself was similar to what others described. First,

with the help of her therapist, she broke through her denial, began eating normally again, and regained her healthy body weight. Then she reconstructed what had driven her to the brink, how she had internalized hatred and become extraordinarily cruel to herself. Changing behavior and recognizing its motivation and her own responsibility led her to mourn her losses, and then to forgive herself for the suffering she had brought upon herself.

"I was grief stricken over the pain I'd created and had to live through, for having been my own torturer. I grieved over letting my body become my battleground, using it for things that were really emotional. I had to ask my body to forgive me for deeply harming it. I had to accept that I didn't want a brilliant career, feeling so humiliated that I'd failed these expectations, and that it was okay. I grieved for the lost years of pleasure, all the scallop breading I didn't eat—it's so sad, this harshness toward myself; I annihilated myself in my desperation to please. Meditation helped me tolerate my grief without running away."

As a woman who had almost died trying to follow other people's instructions, Nancy rejects the pervasive pressure society exerts on people to forgive, as well as attempts to program the response. "If somebody said, 'This is what you have to do to bring forgiveness into your life,' it wouldn't work for me; because I'm so reactive, that would feel like compliance and following orders once more. For me, forgiving myself is a by-product of coming into my own and my deepening understanding—more shades of gray than bells and whistles. This soft awareness of forgiveness is more my style."

Although Nancy rejected the career preordained for her, in the fifteen years since she conquered her anorexia she has chosen one for herself and made a success of it. "Here I am as a professional person," she said, pointing to a confident, attractive photo of herself in a suit, briefcase in hand.

The last picture Nancy showed me, taken recently, was the best. She was also nude in this one, but now she had a sensuous, womanly body bathed in golden light. "I'm glad I have these photos, all of them. Otherwise I would have lost a piece of myself, and it's an important piece." Reclaiming your entire life, including its ghastly aspects, is essential for the ongoing self-forgiveness in which we must all engage.

DEMURE, elegant interior decorator Brenda Lane no more conformed to my stereotype of a whore than Jack O'Reilly had fit my notion of a murderer. In our first psychotherapy session twelve years ago, she had with unspeakable shame confessed her past to me, and for the longest time I was the only person who knew—other than her former boyfriend, who had acted as her pimp.

Brenda had come from a prosperous California family. Her parents, while not overtly cruel, were incapable of giving emotional sustenance or the slightest sense of direction to their six children. In her early twenties, Brenda moved across the country with a much older man, who devised the idea of her working as a part-time call girl to supplement his income. "For the first time in my life someone was telling me what to do, even if it was to jump off a cliff," she told me. After two years of furtively walking into hotels to meet her johns—nobody ever questioned her because of how respectable she looked—she found the life unbearable and abruptly left town. Ten years later, when she finally had a good job and a loving relationship with a man, she came to see me to confront the past she had hidden for so long.

Brenda and I spent five years deciphering what made her seek love through debasement. In her last session, she summarized with quiet intensity how she came to understand and forgive herself:

"When I see the 'working girls' on street corners I feel only sad, never judgmental. How could I have been able to do that? Looking back, I see that it was partly just not knowing better, and also searching for something—a fantasy relationship like Cinderella. Now my reaction is not shame but grief, like somebody who's gone through drug rehabilitation; I've come to terms. It was twenty years ago. I can't make it go away, but it was only a chapter in my life. I'm fortunate that I have a husband who accepts my past—not that he likes it, but he says, 'This is who you are now; you're another person.' It's not a reflection on me, but a tragedy.

"As I look back today I see it as a terrible thing I was caught up in then, but I got out and moved forward. It no longer influences me. My shame could have followed me forever, like a black cloud, so I feel proud and happy that I've overcome it."

Taking responsibility and blaming yourself are not the same. One facilitates self-forgiveness; the other obstructs it. Feeling the full brunt of the damage you have done yourself is always sickening. But disproportionate self-loathing prevents change and feeds on itself. Brenda's inner conviction that she was unworthy of love predated the prostitution and partially motivated her to engage in it. She needed to modify an excessive sense of guilt. Compassion was the missing element that therapy helped supply.

The impetus for forgiving self or others can be equally elusive. Something from the past permits one person to make use of experiences that someone else in similar circumstances cannot. Jack's mentor held up the mirror for other prisoners as well, and few reformed. Not many homeless gang members become ministers after witnessing violence as Dan Snyder did; most are impressed and want to emulate it. When change happens, there is often some childhood experience to build on—in Jack's case, perhaps his father's deathbed gesture of acceptance and forgiveness—moments of kindness or caring a person may not even register consciously, but which exert a subliminal beneficent influence.

Forgiving yourself is active, heightened self-acceptance, based on more than simply tolerating character traits you wish you did not have—in my case, a tendency to be pessimistic, exacting, or overly anxious. You have to face terrible truths about yourself. Because aggressive impulses and destructive behavior are universal, no human being is exempt from committing serious wrongs against the self or others, even if you never murder anybody, prostitute yourself, or join a gang. Holding yourself accountable, without hatred or denial, for the damage you do to the person in the mirror is the prerequisite for every other act of forgiveness.

8

False Forgiveness: The Flight from Rage and Grief

FORGIVING oneself or another is hard and scary; no wonder people try to take short cuts. Pervasive social pressure to forgive, coupled with the difficulty of genuinely doing it, has encouraged an epidemic of false forgiveness in American life, public as well as private.

Politicians and celebrities caught in compromising positions (sexual and otherwise) routinely ask to be pardoned when they don't mean it; people oblige even when they don't believe it. This ritual, though commonplace, is not innocuous; to condone fake contrition is to be implicated in perpetuating it. Colluding with insincerity breeds insincerity, until no one can recognize or experience genuine emotions. Forgiveness is then reduced to the level of psychobabble, where it joins other formerly serious concepts like "healing" and "sharing." This sort of forgiveness has about as much connection to the real thing as fruit-flavored Life Savers do to fruit or to saving lives. Deep and important transactions are cheapened and rendered empty, robbed of their passion and their pain by the way they are reflexively evoked.

Forgiving falsely, whether within oneself, in intimate relationships, or in the outside world, has serious consequences. What happens in the public sphere infiltrates standards for private life, and vice versa. Over time, the practice becomes compulsory and ubiquitous. It damages the ability to distinguish false from true; worse, it destroys the urge to care about the difference. Emotional authenticity as a person or as a nation is lost.

Even those who are not being manipulated by cynical politicians give lip service to forgiveness in their own lives, often unawares. They go through the motions because the emotions aroused by real forgiveness—or real unforgiveness—are too threatening. People who make it their business not to take offense, even when they should, must mute or obliterate the anguished moral struggle others feel. For them, forgiving is not a choice but a compulsion, a solution rather than a resolution.

In the right circumstances, anyone can be prey to the denial and self-deception that lead to false forgiveness; I certainly was as an adolescent. The usual method is to negate that you were wronged in the first place or to rationalize the transgression away. "My father's gambling was simply there, like cold in the winter," a man explained to me. "It was nothing to be upset about." Janice Cooper, a forty-year-old graphic designer whose father sold pornographic photographs through the mail as a sideline to his film developing business, glossed over his crime with a dismissive "Nobody's perfect." But while such people reach the same conclusions as genuine forgivers, nothing changes psychically. They bypass recognizing and judging the transgressor's actions, deny their own negative emotions, and move quickly to heal damage they barely admit they sustained. In their rush to reinterpret, false forgivers short-circuit the reengagement and recognition phases of the resolution process. They never really come to terms.

Automatic and pseudoforgiveness are distinct but related afflictions, and those who favor one are prone to commit the other. Both involve avoidance, rationalization, minimization, or blaming something or someone other than the culprit; "uncontrollable circumstances" are especially popular. False forgivers truly believe that they have forgiven wrongs or that nothing serious befell them, but their motives are suspect. "Professional" forgivers who cultivate a morally superior attitude toward those they have supposedly absolved, and revel in their own goodness, and long-suffering masochists who extract payment for their tolerance, also belong in this category. Compulsive forgivers do acknowledge wrongs, but immediately mask or neutralize their reactions. A man who received an incriminating letter about his father told me he had locked it in a drawer and decided to think about the contents "a few years from now."

Those who employ either strategy harbor considerable residual anger or resentment, whether they know it or not. Though their sincerity is not in doubt, their explanations are superficial or self-justifying. "Forgive and forget," they say. "You can't blame people forever"—as though this were the only alternative to never blaming them at all. They become defensive when confronted with their own contradictions or unexamined assumptions;

false forgivers were the only people I interviewed who always wanted to change the subject and "move on."

The motives for false forgiveness and authentic forgiveness are the same: to maintain ties, to put aside anger, to identify with an ideal or distinguish oneself from a bad example. In false forgiveness, however, fear and avoidance take precedence—fear of anger and sorrow and avoidance of the supposedly dangerous consequences of not forgiving. False forgivers seek to prevent themselves from losing important relationships or from behaving in morally unacceptable or uncontrollable ways. Lying is less painful than telling the truth, and the most effective lie is the one you forget you're telling yourself.

The same people who rail against unforgiveness inadvertently promote imitation forgiveness, which does as much damage and is more insidious. Permanent self-estrangement is the price of both.

PEOPLE who have suffered too many losses forgive falsely to prevent any more. Eva Denis forced herself to put aside shocking wrongs in order to survive the only way she knew how. In her youth, she had fled Hungary during the Holocaust, entrusting cherished possessions to a dear friend. The friend was less than enthusiastic to learn that Eva had survived and was coming home to claim her property after the war and had the audacity to tell Eva so when she arrived. Despite this outrageous reception, Eva did not sever relations with the one person left who reminded her of her past; in fact, she did her old chum a favor, and on her return to the United States sent the woman cosmetics unavailable in Hungary as requested.

They still correspond, though Eva has never received an apology.

Why did she not shun so monstrous a companion? "I can and I must forgive and forget," Eva replied. "If I didn't follow this philosophy I wouldn't have any friends. I survived the Nazis, but I'm still a stranger in America. I tell myself that if I remember the bad I will always be all by myself. I bury and block out things I don't want to think about—not an easy thing to do, but I trained myself. It's sad to talk about the past; I couldn't handle it otherwise."

Even now, years later and in her eighties, Eva lives by the same credo and forces herself immediately to blot out things people do that make her angry. "I have a very small circle of friends as it is, and I don't want to reduce the number," she explained. "If somebody insults me I never complain. I talk to myself and call back an hour later as if nothing happened. I don't want to lose anybody else; it's not worth it. You can only make friends when you're young."

I asked Eva how she would have behaved if her Hungarian friend had requested something expensive or inconvenient to obtain. She hesitated, but admitted that there is virtually nothing she would not have done for old time's sake. Her defensive behavior has to be consistent to work at all.

Eva's dislocation was traumatic, but her reaction is a product of who she is; not every Holocaust survivor would behave similarly. She accepts the terms of the bargain she made with herself without examining the assumptions that support it—whether it really is impossible to make friends in one's later years, and why she is so sure that she would automatically lose any friend she confronted. She is more psychologically alone than she realizes because of, not in spite of, her forced forgiveness; she disconnects herself from her true feelings. Anger does not disappear when it is suppressed. It only reappears in disguise.

FALSE forgivers flee anger as much as loneliness. Mark Epstein, an American lawyer born after World War II, shares Eva Denis's "forgive and forget" philosophy. The only way Mark believes that he can put injuries behind him—and avoid becoming an embittered, disgruntled grudge collector like his father—is to suppress his memories, to internalize his pain and hostility, and to convert these feelings into physical symptoms. He did this years ago when a vindictive cousin brought him up before the state bar on groundless ethics charges, and more recently when his adopted daughter repudiated him publicly.

"I forgive everybody, but that's mostly because I forget," Mark said. "The fact of remembering itself negates part of forgiveness—it's a protected harbor for ill will. People think I'm an idiot to act the way I do, but I don't have the energy to maintain resentment. I use it instead to do good and be good." Mark knows the price he pays for his efforts, but defends them anyway. "If I repress, good for me. I wake up in the middle of the night, and I've got ulcers and high cholesterol, but I'm happier not resenting people; it's one of my values." He assumes anger would fester and last forever unless he took drastic measures to eradicate it—measures he considers necessary to be an honorable and affable man. The psychological distress of anticipating resentment is more toxic than the physical ills Mark suffers because he negates it; his ideals matter more to him than his health.

GRANTING others automatic pardon is a way to guarantee one's own moral behavior toward them. Karen Shepherd excuses things that would outrage most people because she fears how she would act if she did not. Karen's seventeen-year-old stepdaughter Ricky ran off with a fugitive drug dealer and lived on the lam with him. When she resurfaced on Karen's doorstep, Karen took in the couple and their two illegitimate daughters and supported them all until they vanished again, leaving her feeling exploited and frantic about the children. "I can't blame Ricky," she told me. "If I let myself get angry and to get over being angry, I might not be able to set my feelings aside and help her instantly the way I need to; I can't afford to get mad at her; I focus it all on her boyfriend."

Although she still shields Ricky, Karen's feelings are closer to the mark than they used to be. When the couple first disappeared, she reserved her outrage exclusively for the federal agents whom she insisted were pursuing Ricky's boyfriend on trivial charges. Karen deflects and controls her own legitimate righteous wrath and foregoes properly attributing blame in order to avoid being guilty of depraved indifference herself.

False forgiveness is a pattern established early in life. The current crisis is not the first time Karen has forcibly suppressed disruptive emotions; extending an extraordinarily generous benefit of the doubt in the face of extreme or outrageous behavior became habitual with her long ago.

Karen grew up with a fanatical tyrant of a father who

refused to let his daughter accept a scholarship to a prestigious university because he feared the corrupting effects of higher education. When Karen was twenty-one, her mother insisted as a condition of divorce that he confess to his daughter his secret life as a transvestite.

To hear Karen talk, a revelation that would have shocked anyone had virtually no impact on her and produced no scars or negative feelings other than increased sympathy for her father and fury at her mother. "It was not that big a thing in my life. The way he tried to subjugate me was far more significant. And I only recently realized that if he'd really been a controlling bastard he would have locked me in the basement and never let me leave home at all." As for his confession, "The only way for him to get attention in his family was to become female, because his father paid more attention to my aunt."

It is inconceivable that such a disclosure would have little psychological effect on a young woman's sexuality or her view of men. Karen's explanation normalizes her father's pathology and explains it away without considering that many boys whose fathers prefer their sisters find less drastic solutions than cross-dressing. Karen was too troubled by this unwanted information to process it; the sympathy she extended to her father partly served to distract her from the implications of his behavior for her own life—and since he had been so insanely strict with her, his humiliation must have caused her secret vengeful pleasure, which she was expiating. Real compassion is a product of understanding, not a substitute for it.

Many compulsive forgivers have periodic insight into themselves, which they opt not to pursue. Karen explained the motivation behind her relentless emphasis on the positive and her escape from the darker side of her own and other people's natures. With logic similar to Eva's, she said, "Going through the aging process shows me how crucial it is to remember things favorably or neutrally. I used to think it's most important to be honest, but saving your life is what really counts the most." Unlike her own father, she protects her stepdaughter from anger and its consequences—a stepdaughter she probably identifies with, who also rebelled against parental authority, but with far less justification. Karen compulsively forgives Ricky in order to be a better parent than she herself had—all the while minimizing how bad her own actually was.

Suspending judgment originally may have been essential for emotional survival, but it becomes a reflex. Preventing your own potentially immoral behavior inadvertently forces you to tolerate it in others. Those who never judge anybody never truly forgive anybody.

PARENTS tend to exonerate their own children more easily and unquestioningly than they do anybody else; they also hold grudges against those who harm their children longer. To do so is part of most people's definition of the role; as Mark Epstein said, "I'm her father, and fathers forgive." Youth, dependency, the parent's wish to maintain a loving relationship, the closeness of the bond, and its lifelong nature—as well as the intensity of the anger that is stirred up and needs to be managed regularly—determine this course of action. Forgiving quickly, however, is not the same as forgiving automatically; even one's child can, and should, be held accountable. Ac-

knowledging an offense does not preclude lovingly overlooking it afterward.

Just as parents try to excuse their children's actions,
children are too quick to overlook their parents' serious
wrongdoing. "He did the best he could" was the way
Janice Cooper exonerated her father the film-developer/
pornographer. "Everybody in the business did what he
did in those days; money was scarce," she told me. Her
formulation, like Karen's, combines two suspicious elements: she has internalized the maxim that since nobody's
perfect, we should not judge other people's shortcomings,
particularly our parents', and she has accepted her father's
self-justification—common among psychopaths—that ab-
solves him of guilt and obscures the antisocial nature of
his behavior. Her premature conclusion begs the question
of how a daughter feels when the best her father could
do really is not good enough; how can the actions of an
unrepentant pornographer and crook fail to have a negative
impact on his family, and on his daughter's love relationships? If Janice recognizes that her rationalization is
masquerading as forgiveness, she may indeed come to
terms with her father. Then "the best he could do" will
have a different and deeper meaning for her, as my father's flawed life came to have for me; it will include his
criminality, rather than gloss over it.

The desire for closure that motivates false forgivers is
real, but their tactics are suspect. Eva swallows her anger,
Mark somatizes his, and Karen deflects and explains hers
away. Like people afraid of heights who become moun-
tain climbers, they rush precipitously into forgiveness in
order to flee from fear. While this strategy can be superficially effective, it deprives them of discovering that fear

can be faced, and that the consequences are rarely as terrible as anticipated. Would Eva really forfeit all companionship if she expressed herself, or would Mark be hardened by his rage? It is hard to believe that an ethical person like Karen would abandon her stepgrandchildren *in extremis* even if she were furious or indifferent to their mother.

False forgivers are pessimists who look like optimists. They believe that when anger is conscious it becomes endless and dangerous, that registering betrayal leads ineluctably to eternal vengefulness and uncontrollable hatred, and that forgiveness must be forced or it will never happen at all. They are ruled by their need to flee from rage and grief.

Although counterfeit forgiveness maintains relationships, protects the self and others from anger, and permits people to weather crises, those who pass it off as the real thing lose what matters most. Not examining yourself becomes a way of life—and it landed Mark in the hospital with a perforated ulcer.

Forgiveness comes in authentic and ersatz varieties. The instant type obstructs the difficult route to self-knowledge that alone can be liberating; the only way out of pain is through it. In a society that places so high a premium on forgiveness at any cost, the imitations are often encouraged, applauded, and mistaken for the real thing.

9
The Unforgivable I: The Outraged and the Disengaged

AMERICANS demonize not forgiving as much as they idealize forgiving. False forgiveness, the quick fix of easy peace, and the emotional inauthenticity that springs from them have proliferated as a result. We don't even know we're missing anything.

Forgiveness has become spiritually correct. The resident swami at a yoga ashram in Manhattan's East Village offers sessions on "Cultivating Forgiveness." "Anger is armor around the heart which constricts the capacity to love" reads the ad. A friend of mine who discovered a month earlier that his lover had been unfaithful was warned by a solicitous acquaintance that "every second you hold on to anger kills thousands of years of karma." Fortunately, these drastic penalties are easy to avoid. A program on daytime TV called *Forgive and Forget* presents guests who resolve grievances in an hour and provides them bouquets to bestow on the newly forgiven. A catalog I received recently featured a "Forgiveness Candle," evidently to help resentments go up in aromatherapeutic smoke. So deeply has the forgiveness mystique penetrated our culture that the prestigious Templeton Foundation, a charitable trust more wealthy than Nobel that funds studies in religion and society, was inundated with proposals from behavioral scientists when it announced it was offering grants for "forgiveness studies."

With all the contemporary emphasis on diversity, there is curiously little tolerance for multiple perspectives or divergence from this agenda. The culture of Forgiveness Lite, which now extends far beyond the rigors of the traditional religious position, inhibits analysis and offers little comfort to dissenters. It has been espoused with self-serving enthusiasm by public figures who hope to avoid condemnation for reprehensible behavior. When something is assumed to be a universal good, nobody asks when it makes sense and when it would be disastrous, problematic, or impossible.

Some of the most admirable people I know have not forgiven on occasion. Part of what makes them exceptional is precisely this—that they think for themselves, understand the complexity of emotional life, and know the difference between love and its imposters. They are also the most forgiving people I know.

Not forgiving needs to be reconceived. It is not an avoidance of forgiveness or a retreat into paranoia, but a legitimate action in itself, with its own progression, motivation, and justification. This concept is so new and so alien to current trends that we have no name for it. Nonetheless, there are many circumstances in which it is the proper and most emotionally authentic course of action. Vengeance, with which it is usually equated, is something else entirely, a perversion of genuine unforgiveness just as false forgiveness is a parody of real forgiveness.

To withhold forgiveness for the right reasons is a decision as hard-won as to grant it. For *moral unforgivers*, refusing means telling the truth, asserting fundamental rights, and opposing injustice. *Psychologically detached unforgivers* accept the painful reality that they cannot experience the positive internal connection with a betrayer—usually a parent—which forgiving would require. Neither type is vindictive, or against forgiveness in principle; they share the capacity to forgive and do not exercise it indiscriminately.

Moral Unforgivers

Forgiving, presumed to be a panacea, can be poison. "In my family, the very act of forgiveness is an extortion of my soul," declares my colleague Sandy Katz. "It endorses what they did, which was to deny the truth and pressure me to sacrifice myself. For me not to forgive my brother at my parents' behest is my self-affirmation."

Sandy's parents had looked the other way when her violent bully of an older brother thrust a screwdriver up her rectum—even when he set her on fire. "Afterward they didn't leave tools or matches lying around, but they never acknowledged what he did to me. He continued to behave this way and they continued to insist that I submit; my mother would say, 'He's just trying to get close to you because he doesn't know how to be friends.' She'd confuse me by saying it was all out of love, and I had no recourse."

Parents define a child's world; there is no escape. Unsure of their own reality, children who have no validation and no protection become prisoners mentally as well as physically. Not forgiving is a recourse they can create only as independent adults, a way to free themselves from years of being coerced to agree that hate is really love.

Under the pretense of promoting family harmony, parents who need to deny one child's viciousness and their own negligence often try to force the victimized child to be "mature" and "rise above it." These more intact, "good" siblings continue to make the same demands of themselves. Their willingness to accept bad treatment, to feel they deserve it, or to define it out of existence then extends beyond their families and damages their later lives. Even those in less extreme circumstances tend to absorb parental values as an unexamined template for their own responses, making it difficult for them to distinguish what they truly feel from what has been imposed upon them.

Ten years ago, at age thirty-five, Sandy finally defied her parents by refusing her brother's phone calls. "I started getting guilt-inducing messages from them saying that I was abandoning him and destroying the family. They became increasingly angry and accusatory, haranguing me to forgive and forget without admitting there was anything to forgive and forget. I wrote him a note detailing what he had done to me and said I wouldn't speak to him until he was willing to acknowledge it. He sent back a letter taking the moral high ground: that he was just as hurt as I, that all children fight—as if these were normal childhood squabbles—and that he was willing to let bygones be bygones. Why couldn't I?"

Sandy hasn't attended a family function with her

brother since she received that letter. "I've taken a strong position that he's out of my life, even though my parents still try to bully me into capitulating. I know it's difficult for them to have two separate sets of holidays, but I forbid them to talk to me about it because their pollyanna attitude enrages me."

The moral unforgiver makes a distinction between the extreme circumstances where a relationship must be severed and other, more commonplace, injuries. "It's not so much what my brother did as a child, but what he continues to be as a man that I find unacceptable," Sandy explained. "He never changed, never grew, and just found new ways to feel entitled. It would only be right to forgive what he did as a child—it would be legitimate and healthy for everybody. But it would be wrong not to hold him responsible for being an undeveloped person now; I would be colluding in creating a false reality, which was what allowed me to be violated in the first place."

Forgiveness as defined by a family with something to hide negates a daughter's right to think and feel for herself; what they consider healing would in fact be self-annihilating. "I refuse to participate in their denial," Sandy said. "It condones evil. False forgiveness allows evil to be excused and perpetuated; people have to be held accountable. Making up without apology or remorse would have been another degradation of myself." Any course of action that is forced upon one person by another, for the supposed benefit of another, compromises the humanity of everyone involved, rather than enhancing it, as forgiveness is always presumed to do.

Paradoxically—and contrary to the conventional wisdom—refusing to forgive or have further contact with an unrepentant, abusive relative is therapeutic. "My lack of forgiveness has not impeded my development or my relationships at all; in fact, it's cured me," she said. "Before I took a stand I was always depressed and acceding to others' needs, always confused about my rights and about what was real. My parents' requirement that I forgive my brother was an excuse for him to continue what he did; forgiveness as it got framed by them meant being invalidated forever. I'm so relieved that I've repudiated this. I've never had a moment's regret." It is commonly assumed that forgiving promotes mental health and alleviates depression. But doing the opposite can express a person's very right to live.

Responsible unforgivers are never antiforgiveness; Sandy regularly forgives outside her family, even when the offender fails to apologize. "In a good relationship— not a perfect relationship—it's different; how bad are the screwups? If the person is still loving enough it comes naturally." By recognizing the distinction between actions worthy and unworthy of tolerance, and upholding her own moral point of view, a child triumphs over the masochistic role her family assigned to her. Her insistence on truth and justice, which lead her to refuse to forgive, is the foundation of her sense of self.

Judging a disturbed and brutal sibling can provoke enormous distress, particularly when religious scruples and the wish to please at all costs reinforce parental pleas to reconcile. Katie Randolph, a soft-spoken art student not given to hyperbole, had a "turbulent and horrifying" adolescence. After her mother died when Katie was thirteen, her father was frequently away on business, leaving her the virtual hostage of her older brother, a two-hundred-pound "violent recluse" who menaced her with a gun, locked her out of the house in winter, and stole her money. As is typical in these situations, Mr. Randolph blamed his daughter rather than his son, and Katie accepted responsibility in an effort to please him. "When I complained to my father about the theft, he said 'Why didn't you hide it—you know how he is.' I've always had to do everything for myself, and always had to give in to him." Forgiving her brother would feel like more of the same.

A teenager left to fend for herself is her father's victim as well as her brother's. Her father's efforts to reunite his children are motivated not by concern for his daughter's welfare, but by his need to absolve himself of responsibility for what happened to her. Any parent who conceals his own guilt under the beneficent guise of fostering forgiveness is committing an act of emotional reabandonment.

For four years, Katie has resisted her father's admonishments, but her Christian upbringing, her tendency to be a compliant caretaker, and guilt about doing better than her brother (which the more stable sibling always feels), shake her resolve. "To forgive him I have to submit to him yet again, to deny that anything ever happened. It's up to me to make our family perfect; I'm the bad one if I don't. I've worked so hard, and he's done nothing to help himself. My religion says it's wrong not to forgive—but why should I unless he comes to me and says 'I'm trying, I'm so sorry'?"

No emotion that has not first been acknowledged can be altered voluntarily. Therefore, only when one sibling feels free to refuse to be the keeper of the other can she develop an independent identity—a prerequisite for offering genuine forgiveness to him or to anyone else.

Unlike vengefulness, real unforgiveness is a dynamic state of mind. In early adulthood, not forgiving is a natural way to counteract childhood victimization. In maturity, the need to protest frequently diminishes. Katie may pardon her brother later, or forge a relationship with her family that is not based on compliance or self-abnegation, as Sandy Katz has done.

After we met, Katie wrote me a letter:

Our talk brought a lot to light about how terrible I feel because I choose not to forgive my brother. Now I can see that my decision makes sense. If my brother decides to help himself, then it will be his gift to himself. As for me, I'm going to concentrate on not feeling guilty and sad.

Feelings of sadness and guilt accompany the decision not to accede to the expectations of others; the person who needs forgiveness is not the perpetrator, but the unforgiver.

Not forgiving is hardest within a family, because few people find it easy to sever so important a tie. They struggle between losing their relatives and losing themselves, and are tormented by their knowledge that their action is viewed as a betrayal by the very people by whom they have been betrayed.

Choosing not to forgive is as least as difficult as forgiving because it is so unpopular and contrary to convention. Unforgivers are seen as rebels or ingrates, lacking in family feeling or moral values. Having the courage of your convictions may make you proud and strong; it may also make you lonely and anxious.

Despite what universal forgiveness advocates proclaim, forgiving without reconciling is often impossible in families. The superficially appealing theoretical distinction between the two actions—that a relationship need be resumed only in reconciliation—dissolves in practice when both parties are alive and expected to be in contact with each other. Parents want their aggrieved children to act differently, not just to feel differently, celebrating holidays and attending family functions with their unrepentant tormenters for the rest of their lives. These occasions repeat childhood traumas because everybody is required to pretend that everything is fine and that the past is forgotten or unimportant. Such forced reconciliation is precisely what family members who foist forgiveness on reluctant relatives desire. In such cases, resistance is justified. Not recognizing the inextricable link between forgiveness and reconciliation in pathological families is sophistical and dangerous.

A major component of a relationship can sometimes be repudiated without severing the whole; partial unforgiveness is as common as partial forgiveness, and as frequently ignored—yet another effect of the widespread tendency to polarize the two.

Paul Thompson's born-again Christian parents pray that mutual forgiveness as they define it will yield more than occasional holiday dinners with their son; they want him to gainsay his identity and accept their condemnation. Even though he is gay, they say, they are proud of him and welcome him as a member of the family. The

Thompsons are founding members of Return, Incorporated, an international evangelical organization dedicated to converting gay people to heterosexuality. They insist that they "hate the sin and love the sinner;" why can't Paul appreciate their concern for his salvation and accept their forgiveness?

Until they announced at a recent press conference that "Our son's homosexuality is worse than a death in the family," Paul managed to maintain an uneasy truce with his parents; fear of the destructive power of his own rage, coupled with an unconscious belief that they might be right, prevented a confrontation. His implicit acceptance of their terms perpetuated mutual false forgiveness. "But now," he told me, "they've raised the stakes too high. They actually said that my being gay was a fate worse than death—in essence, that they would rather I had died. When my boyfriend and I broke up and I was devastated, my mother said it was 'an answered prayer.' They deny that what they're doing is personal and that it's damaging to me; this is hatred masked as love. I won't go any further; it's more a process of mourning than of forgiving them."

Paul's parents' entrenched, sanctimonious refusal to admit their hostility is a nonnegotiable obstacle to full reconciliation. For them to disapprove of his sexual orientation is one thing; to wage a conversion campaign while insisting that they are acting out of compassion alone is another.

Without asking his son's permission, Mr. Thompson wrote and self-published *Psalms for Sorrowing Parents*, a book that included intimate letters his son had written to him. "I sobbed when he gave me a copy," Paul said. He refused his father's subsequent request to be pardoned for invading his privacy, the only offense Mr. Thompson would ever admit. "I won't do it because it's just a ritual for him, not blood and guts. Real forgiveness has to be based on working to change; he wants me to forgive him for what he's going to keep doing." Granting his father's wish would minimize and obscure the nature of the conflict between them, eliminating the possibility of an honest exchange.

In the complex relations between parents and children, affection and hostility and pride and disappointment always coexist. To label an ongoing transgression unforgivable does not necessarily obliterate all positive ties. "Despite their fanaticism, fundamentally they love me very deeply," Paul acknowledged—and he knows he loves them too. Therefore, although he will not underwrite his parents' behavior by forgiving it, neither will he abandon them in retaliation; mature separation is not amputation. He has decided to maintain occasional contact with them, provided Return, Incorporated is not mentioned. "Complete detachment isn't any more healthy than fusion—but I won't be careful or quiet any longer. Now I must respond out of my own truth."

Partial nonforgiveness requires a person to bear alone the burden of intense ambivalence and continuing grief. The illusion of family harmony is lost forever, but it is replaced with something limited, painful, and real.

Proponents of universal forgiveness refuse to recognize that moral unforgivers exist. They find it inconceivable that unforgiving victims of injustice could be outraged but not obsessed by their injuries, that they could even sympathize or retain conditional connections with those they refuse to pardon. The black-and-white terms in which forgiveness and its opposite are defined cannot account for the way that forgiveness may hide malign motives and produce destructive results—or that saying no can be an act of self-affirmation and liberation.

Psychologically Detached Unforgivers

"The Ten Commandments," Orthodox Jewish convert Rebecca Sachs had reminded me, "tells us to 'Honor Thy Father and Thy Mother'—and not just if they've been nice and sober." Father Neuhaus had spoken of the "natural bonds of responsibility," to even the worst mother, which require a child to "do all you can, and pray for the grace to love her." A child can come to realize that a neglectful alcoholic mother was incapacitated rather than uncaring, that a self-indulgent playboy who abdicated parental responsibility has a warm heart, and that a heedless, philandering father like mine was also a nurturing and inspiring one.

There are, however, parents who deserve condemnation rather than honor, who have failed so utterly that any redeeming features are buried, lost, or simply not enough to outweigh the harm they caused. Loving them again is an impossible task. Betrayal of this magnitude can occur in any intimate relationship, but is most devastating when committed by parents against children. It is a major accomplishment for these sons and daughters to cease to hate; with rare exceptions, for the sake of their own emotional survival, they can do no more.

For a daughter to be unloved by her mother may be the worst betrayal of all, since mother love is supposed to be the most inalienable, and the same sex parent is the primary source of a child's identity. Like ancient legal codes that specified no penalties for parricide because it was an unthinkable crime—the myth of Oedipus notwithstanding—contemporary culture worships mother love and refuses to see mother hate, although the unspeakable proof of its potency is thrust in our faces every day. Malevolent mothers are explained away as criminals or lunatics and never live next door. Societal pressure to avoid the awful truth that maternal cruelty, mental as well as physical, is far more common than we care to know makes coming to terms with its effects more difficult for those who have endured it.

Even women who have forgiven much find this aberration impossible to overcome. Neither Dana Reinhardt nor Jessica Kramer will ever forgive their mothers, though Dana invites her alcoholic ex-husband for Christmas and Jessica loves her father despite his suicide. Both had truly terrible mothers who displayed an eerily similar combination of coldness and cruelty toward their daughters. Although Jessica and Dana were equally horrified by their sentiments at the time, they felt relief when their mothers died and have never missed them.

"She was unnatural, a freak of nature," Dana told me. "She committed the unforgivable—she hated me. She was really a bad, evil, person, who was actively cruel to a child. I remember that she told me once 'I can't understand how I could have had such an ugly daughter.' I was a terrible mistake."

"She was cold, uninvolved, and rejecting and never interested in me," said Jessica. "By age five I had given up on her. I was never sure whether she hated me or was just indifferent. I was a burden and a competitor."

Both Dana and Jessica were unwanted children of loveless marriages, and each bright, engaging little girl looked to others for the basics. As long as their mothers lived, they mistreated their daughters. Mrs. Reinhardt barely fed Dana and ripped books from her hands when she tried to read. Her malice was consistent and relentless; even when she was dying, and Dana approached her kindly at a family gathering, she made a withering remark. Mrs. Kramer was so detached from Jessica that she was surprised to notice that her twenty-eight-year-old daughter was left-handed, and so mean-spirited that she used the money earmarked for Jessica's education to speculate in real estate with the son of the man she married after Jessica's father killed himself.

Damage this deep takes years to undo. Dana battled depression most of her adult years. "Being her child made me not trust people who said they loved me," she said. "I had a large family in reaction; I wanted to be the best mother in the world." Jessica still worries about her competence and lovability. "Having her as my mother makes me anxious about being a mother myself, as if I should say, 'Please forgive me, I don't know what this is like' to my own daughters. I'm afraid that my experience with her limits my ability to be intimate with other people; as a result, I became involved with women who did not wish me well." They express these fears matter-of-factly, with an unflinching awareness of what lacking maternal devotion has cost them.

Those who reject wicked mothers are the loneliest and most censured of the unforgivers because they violate a

taboo by calling attention to a deeply disturbing phenomenon. Therefore, these unloved children initially always
blame themselves for their mothers' inability to respond
and condemn themselves for despising their mothers. As
Dana put it, "When you say 'I can't stand my mother,'
people think it's not natural. Everybody loves her own
mother—but everybody else's mother loves her." Jessica
said, "I was finally able to cry over my father's death, but
never over hers. When she died of cancer when I was
thirty-eight, I was mostly glad to be rid of her. But afterward I felt terrible about my indifference, even more than
about my earlier hatred." As I had experienced myself,
hatred of a parent who has betrayed you feels disturbing
but justified, while coldness seems more a reflection of
something abnormal about you. In Jessica's case, since her
hatred was unalloyed with love and her indifference
deeper than mine ever was, her guilt was far more intense
than mine. "I thought I felt what only the evil feel," she
confessed.

A curative relationship in adulthood is often necessary
to help an unloved daughter separate from her mother
and convert hatred and self-hatred into sober recognition
and compassion for herself. She must learn that her feelings are justified and no reflection on her. Jessica's therapist and Dana's second husband Tom provided the
necessary nurturing. "I used to wonder what I could have
done to deserve her treatment, because it made no sense,"
Dana recounted. "In the process of telling Tom I realized
she was bad and it had nothing to do with me. In trying
to make it comprehensible to him I made it comprehensible to myself. That's when I stopped being depressed; the

person I finally forgave was myself; now I hardly think about her.''

Friends can be more worthy of love than ungiving family members. "I was devastated when a close friend died soon after my mother did," Jessica recalled. She was doubly devastated when she realized how much more deeply she grieved for her friend than she had for her mother. In a process that paralleled the one I went through when I compared my responses to my father's and my analyst's deaths, Jessica's reaction to this second loss made her question her own character; what kind of a daughter—what kind of a human being—was she? "To mourn my friend and not my mother seemed like what a monster feels. It was a shining moment when my analyst said 'It's okay to love your friend more than your mother.' What had been disturbing me was not so much that she didn't love me but that *I* didn't love *her*. Not loving her meant I was like her, a person incapable of love. When I realized that I didn't love her *because* she didn't love me, I understood that I could still love. I haven't forgiven her, but I'm not angry any more; she had some nice qualities, like liveliness. But in the most important way she was never really my mother."

In the conventional view, the decision to forgive must not be based on whether the perpetrator deserves it; only then can the independent will of the victim be guaranteed. In fact, refusing to forgive a heartless mother expresses a daughter's right to her own feelings; it does not perpetuate her mother's power over her. Recognizing that you are under no obligation to profess love you do not feel is a hard-won freedom.

Forgiveness can have an ominous meaning for those

who have been the objects of ongoing, intentional mis-treatment. A toxic parent-child relationship is not so much a "natural bond," as an unnatural bondage that must be repudiated.

Being their mothers' daughters has not destroyed Dana or Jessica and does not dominate their lives as adults. With work and with help, they have come to temper their hatred and tolerate their indifference. But, as Dana observed, "Understanding doesn't always bring forgiveness."

ANYBODY who struggles with intimate betrayal must re-engage with the experience, actively choosing to think and to feel what was once unbearable. The genuine separation that psychologically detached unforgivers achieve is one of many possible good outcomes. But aversion, which it superficially resembles, is not. Just as phobics are always obsessed with the objects of their horror, those who amputate a tie to an unforgiven parent only conceal an intense continuing involvement.

Henry Mann, the lawyer whose ailing father died in his arms after years of estrangement, still detests his mother even though he tries to feel as little as he can about her. Time has not altered his visceral reaction. This woman, whom he adored as a little boy, had him sleep in her bed until he was twelve, and tried to prevent him from making friends his own age. "I lived to serve her," he recalled. "Grasping her narcissism is horrifying. I find her totally loathsome as a human being. An awful mother doesn't bear forgiving, just accepting. I want to disconnect from her so completely that I don't want to be engaged even by anger; anger opens the possibility of redemption and understanding." Reconnection in any way with a mother who has violated her child's basic boundaries still endangers his autonomy. A man who says, "I'm still afraid she'll strike at me from the grave," as Henry does, is terrified of the power he attributes to her and unaware of his own strength. Instead of separating, he has erected a mental barrier to prevent himself from being sucked once again into her malign orbit.

Most psychotherapists—including several Henry consulted—would be appalled by such sentiments; members of the profession tend to be passionate propagandists for forgiveness, especially of patients' parents. One therapist predicted that unless Henry forgave his mother, he would "fall into a terrible depression when she died," and encouraged him to pay her a visit, hoping perhaps to rekindle the old flame. Such warnings and literal-minded solutions either estrange patients or encourage feelings that are false at best and dangerous at worst. Instead of trying to transform repulsion into forgivenesss, a therapist must appreciate that it is there for a reason and help the patient investigate its meaning. Forgiving a devouring mother would feel like uncontrollable reimmersion in her body; not forgiving creates room to breathe. Only reexperiencing this fear in all its horrific intensity can neutralize it and lessen the need for extreme measures against it. Phobic avoidance then turns naturally into a more integrated form of unforgiving detachment.

The most valuable help a therapist can offer to someone struggling with forgiveness—or that a person can do alone—is to address the obstacles to reengagement. Fears about the anger that the process always generates require special attention. Henry blocks rage at his vampirelike mother for fear it would lead to intolerable forgiveness; Karen Shepherd neutralizes fury at her wayward step-daughter because she dreads feeling icy indifference when she "gets over being angry." Both were impeded by their fantasies about what reengagement would entail. The actual experience of reengagement, which includes as much sorrow as rage, would be different from what either one anticipates.

No one way of resolving betrayal is right for everyone, even for two people who have superficially similar experiences. Both Henry and documentary filmmaker Maggie Alexander had incestuous mothers, but one forgave and the other never will. A son's secret, sensuous attachment to a mother with whom he was "totally in love" is far more insidious and requires more radical measures to disentangle than a daughter's purely physical contact with a mother who is otherwise unapproachable.

When a parent-child bond has been noxious, psychological removal is a more realistic goal than forgiveness. Henry acknowledged this implicitly when he speculated about how he would want to deal with his mother's aging. "When she gets sick will I suddenly become a son? I won't forgive her but I'll probably take care of her financially." Morality demands responsible behavior, but must not legislate love.

DISENGAGING from a fatally flawed parent sometimes seems to come naturally, without anguish. The very ease with which some people reject their parents is disquieting, since it violates the stereotype of filial devotion. Can it be real?

Biochemist Annie Travers remembers never feeling

anything but contempt or worse for her father. He was even the macabre inspiration for her eventual career. "At thirteen, I half-seriously borrowed books on plant toxicology from the library to plot his murder," she merrily confessed. "He was a selfish brute who considered his three children his property. We were his beasts of burden. Once when I was a teenager, he said, 'I can do anything I want with you'—and he would have if my uncle hadn't threatened to call the police." Annie's uncle, a blind biologist who lived with the family, was her protector, mentor, and soulmate. "He taught me how to think," she said tenderly.

Annie discussed what must have been a miserable situation with scientific detachment, and not a hint of recrimination. Throughout our interview, she referred to her father as "this guy," and seemed surprised when I asked what qualities she had inherited from him. "I'm my uncle's daughter," she said. A substitute parent saved her from her real one.

Under the right circumstances, a traumatic past can be left behind without being consciously mourned. Living with a beloved, admirable uncle who shared and validated her feelings—something few children in a similar predicament enjoy—made Annie's unusual solution possible. Annie's hatred of her father, unlike Jessica's of her mother, did not seem to her to be "what a monster feels"; it was one of the bonds she shared with her uncle. Still, no daughter is born despising her father; what became of her original love? "You have deep feelings, but they get lost," Annie admitted. "What love there was initially got strangled; he did nothing to keep it." As Annie matured, her fear and hatred evolved into indifference, and though she still speaks of her father with distaste, she is not bitter. "People are much too willing to blame others. Since I moved out thirty years ago, my life has been what I make of it—I'm responsible." A self-reliant attitude, the opposite of vengefulness, circumscribes the influence of a bad father.

Annie was away on a fellowship when her father died, and she had no qualms about not coming back for the funeral; in their last conversation he had berated her for not going to medical school. She grieved deeply when her dear uncle died.

While she has not dealt with all the ramifications, Annie is the first to acknowledge that her father had a negative impact on her life. "Of course it took me a long time to feel men could be trusted, though I think I'm really well adjusted. I'm sorry I didn't have a father, but there are worse things in life—at least I wasn't beaten." Recognizing loss without feeling like a perpetual victim is the earmark of legitimate unforgiveness.

Annie claims never to have been disturbed by her unwillingness to reconcile with her father, alive or dead. "I never felt the slightest need to do it. I always knew we would be better off without him, and my uncle agreed with me. It hasn't been a trauma for me." She is a woman at peace with not being at peace, at a price that does not seem excessive.

Love for a parent cannot die a "natural" death. Since a surrogate parent can only compensate for, but can never actually replace, a father, there is a level of grief for the loss of that original love that Annie has never plumbed. If she ever feels that the dread of dependence that underlies her fierce independence interferes with her ability to be intimate, she may need to reopen what she foreclosed and begin a more active mourning process.

Annie has also been repeatedly warned by friends and therapists that her unforgiving attitude would eventually be her downfall, but she isn't afraid they're right. "People try to convince me that because I didn't make peace with him I'd suffer for it down the line; they feel that something's missing, that there hasn't been closure. I think it's more about them and their own fathers; I'm fine." Although I believe that Annie has not fully grieved for what she never had, she has come to terms in her own way. For others to find her wanting because of what she has not done is an imposition of alien values. It is their problem, not hers.

An unforgivable parent is qualitatively different from a damaged one. It is not what they did but how they did it that makes them beyond redemption in their children's eyes. Calvin Westfield's father deprived his son of many millions of dollars more than Jessica Kramer's mother refused her, and yet Calvin recovered "unconditional love" for him. Jessica's father's suicide was more dramatic than her mother's indifference, but she ultimately wept over his loss and forgave him. Remembered shreds of decency, moments of love or tenderness or empathy, can mitigate almost any horror. Coldness is harder to forgive than cruelty.

Most outraged and disengaged unforgivers are repeatedly lobbied by family members or therapists to override their convictions. Religious sentiment motivates some of these pleas, but most come from self-interest, convenience, and the very human wish to avoid tension. Families invested in denying the very incidents that the unforgiver highlights are loathe to be reminded of them. Despite the evidence, people refuse to believe that hateful deeds can destroy the deepest love of all.

Intent should be the critical factor in determining whether forgiveness is possible or justified. The most culpable person is the one who acts with conscious will to cause harm, or who, though capable of acting differently, inflicts injury anyway. "I'm more forgiving of my mother than my father because he wasn't crazy," one man told me. Extenuating circumstances and life crises, and the rest of the person's behavior, must be factored in; Tammy Kaye was ready to take a chance on her mother, whom she had always hated and considered malevolent, when she began to identify with her and feel sympathy for her plight. The task becomes easier if the offending person has suffered; those who escape unscathed are far more difficult to exonerate. Many people are also willing to extend the benefit of the doubt to someone who cannot admit wrongdoing, but still makes an effort to reform. Anything that can be taken as acknowledgment or apology—any token of humanity—can be acceptable. However, as Annie noted, once love is strangled it rarely breathes again.

Many children who had a poisonous parent identify someone else as their "real" parent, and recognize early in life that, as a patient of mine expressed it, "My father was my enemy." Not trying endlessly to get blood from a stone saved them, and few felt the impulse to embrace the stone. Although this too had effects on their lives, realistically assessing the situation left them better off, and better able to find a substitute caretaker. In these cases, the psychological task is to realize that not forgiving an unloving and unlovable parent does not doom you to repeat that parent's life.

Too often, therapists and others promulgate forgiveness in circumstances where it cannot or should not occur, without considering whether doing so serves their needs or their patients'. When someone is able to pardon a dead or unrepentant offender—Tammy Kaye's mother or David Darielle's lover for example—the impetus comes entirely from within. Sometimes what people really need is permission not to forgive, to feel what they feel. Granting permission need not foreclose resolution; it may be the step that makes it possible.

10

The Unforgivable II: Conflict and Vengeance

Although moral and psychologically detached unforgivers may feel anguish along the way, they usually reach a point of equilibrium once they make their decisions. For many others, explicit or implicit conflicts between feelings, religious principles, ethics, or social responsibilities, never disappear. Negotiating these fundamental contradictions requires serious thought and continuous effort, just as forgiving does.

The *ambivalent unforgiver* is caught between opposing moral and emotional considerations. *Religious unforgivers,* whose faith prescribes universal forgiveness as a moral absolute, find themselves in a quandary: either they must renounce their beliefs, or redefine them. Life experience has caused *reformed forgivers* to reject the conventional attitude they once accepted.

The *vengeful* belong in a separate category. They embody every disturbing characteristic traditionally attributed to all unforgivers—rage, hate, paranoia, and the guiltless desire to destroy. We are all prey, in attenuated form, to the obsessions that consume them.

Ambivalent Unforgivers

Torn between what they feel and what they think, ambivalent unforgivers face chronic inner turmoil. The best they can do is articulate their divided loyalties and try to maintain an uneasy truce with themselves. Their predicament shows that not every dilemma about forgiveness can comfortably be resolved.

Dr. Jonathon Bishop, a child psychiatrist who has been in practice for forty years, cannot find his way out of his own battle over forgiveness despite all his work and all his knowledge. He places enormous value on honor and self-restraint, yet his passionate outrage at his father's humiliating treatment of him in childhood still rankles, and none of his strenuous self-examination makes more than a dent in the pain he feels. "I could never visit his grave, never," this scholarly, opinionated, fiercely loyal man says emphatically. "My father used to tell me I caused my mother's psychotic violence by upsetting her and punished me for it. He called me a coward for crying when I fought back against two bullies even though I have a crippled leg; he used to say 'I have no use for you.' His refusal to admit what happened was like saying the Holocaust didn't happen. He made me too lonely and too responsible. As much as I worry whether my fury is justified, I still hate him for these things. The power of hate is enormous." This healer is haunted by the paradox that he has dedicated his life to exorcising other people's demons while still in thrall to his own.

For Dr. Bishop, to forgive his father would be to disconnect from his past, and he cannot manage to do it; he is not even sure he should try. "I'm still identified with my father—I have a terrible temper like his even though I don't justify it like he did. I can't stand the part of myself that resembles him, but memories are a part of you. You can mitigate their influence, but you can't eradicate them. If I forgive him, I'd be lying, and I believe in truth. To be unforgiving is honest, but to feel as vengeful as I do seems malevolent, neurotic, and dishonorable." His most cherished values make it impossible for him to feel peaceful and courageous simultaneously. "There is always a part of myself I wouldn't be living up to. If I don't get even I'm too weak to get even—that response is visceral. I know this spoils part of my life. It makes me feel bad and burdened even though I've helped so many children, but there are limits to insight. It does what it does, and it doesn't do what it doesn't do."

Although Dr. Bishop's vindictive thoughts trouble him, they do not control him; a genuinely vindictive person would be possessed, rather than distressed.

Dr. Bishop's sober acknowledgment that there is no solution to his conflict contradicts the facile optimism, the fantasy of perfectability, that is a basic assumption of the universal forgiveness movement. That conundrums like his can never be fully resolved is one of the more unpopular and profound contributions psychoanalysis has made to understanding the human condition. Not everything can be repaired, even with the best will in the world; it is not just a matter of trying harder or having a positive attitude or finding the right affirmation. Limitations, born of history and character, make us who we are. To know that some damage can only be contained, never undone, is both tragic and true—as well as strangely comforting. Denying this fact is not just a problem about forgiveness, but about America.

Pioneering feminist writer Lydia Parker has a philosophical debate with forgiveness. She vacillates between two opposing views of the world, both equally central to her vision and her values as a political activist. "I struggle with irreconcilable contradictions on this issue," she said. "The inability to forgive is linked to disbelief in personal change and transformation. I believe we can change things; if I refuse to forgive, it means you are what you did, and thinking that is reprehensible." On the other hand, she feels that in certain circumstances, not forgiving is a moral statement. "I find cruelty and lying in ways that ruin someone's life unacceptable. They are anathema to me. To do these things, repent, and be forgiven cancels out another's suffering. I can't pardon or retract my condemnation. I care about moral boundaries; I don't want to live in a world where nothing is alien to me." Like Dr. Bishop, she risks being untrue to herself whichever side she takes.

If they thought about it, many people would discover within themselves the ambivalence about forgiveness that plagues Lydia Parker and Jonathon Bishop. Their contradictory beliefs can neither be denied nor altered, only acknowledged. Articulating the paradox cannot remove it but can make it easier to live with.

Religious Unforgivers

When I interviewed Rabbi Posner and Father Neuhaus about Jewish and Christian positions on forgiveness, I naïvely assumed that every member of the clergy, every churchgoing Christian, and most devout Jews, would agree with them and feel obliged to forgive under all circumstances. Further investigation revealed a lack of consensus among religious leaders and laity alike.

Some of the pious who refuse to forgive certain people feel no conflict with religious doctrine, while others reject or rebel against their creeds because they were counseled to take actions in the name of forgiveness that harmed them—actions contrary to the principles that the priest and the rabbi expounded to me.

Universal articles of faith are interpreted with remarkable latitude. One regular churchgoer told me that she knew she had pardoned her father for a string of horrific offenses "because I don't hate him," but that she and her mother agreed that they would be better off if he died— a sentiment many would consider sinful. Notions of forgiveness are as subjective among the devout as among the secular; in fact, since forgiveness is compulsory for most believers, they are more likely to soften the compulsion by stretching the definition.

MARY Margaret Morgan came home from work one day after five years of marriage to find her husband, his bags packed, walking out the door. "I need some space" was all he said by way of explanation, and he never spoke to her again. Mary Margaret became dangerously ill from shock and grief, and even went mute for several months.

Two years after her ordeal, I asked this devout Catholic woman with the gilt crucifix on the wall of her lavender-scented living room whether she had forgiven him. "I've never considered it," she replied without hesitation. "What he did is despicable, but I don't know if it's possible to forgive somebody who hasn't asked to be forgiven—otherwise it's a highfalutin' notion. He almost destroyed me and he thinks he hasn't done anything. If I said 'I forgive you' he would laugh at me."

Mary Margaret believes that forgiveness is not a moral duty she must fulfill for her own salvation, but a conditional response to a request that has never been made. Furthermore, rather than being spiritually distressed by her continuing sense of outrage, she considers it justified—a position far removed from Father Neuhaus's admonition to "pray for the grace" to convert anger to love. "I'm comfortable with the angry feeling I have. His behavior is ongoing and not acceptable. I never wanted vengeance, and anger isn't a sin; God gets angry all the time. Sometimes those flames do get fanned and I feel really furious, but not liking what happened is a sign of sanity—particularly since feeling sorry for myself used to be my vocation." Learning to direct anger where it belongs, rather than continuing to absorb it as she did at first, probably saved her life; she does not need to forgive to save her soul.

Forgiveness as she defines it is beyond her jurisdiction. "If I think about forgiving him, inevitably I don't do it. That would be putting myself in a position where I not only pass judgment, but I pass sentence also. Who do I think I am?" This, too, is contrary to Christian doctrine; God alone can pardon sin, but it is always incumbent on the wronged party to grant forgiveness, regardless of whether the betrayer repents.

Without realizing it, Mary Margaret has recast basic Catholic doctrine. Her priest has never pressed her to get rid of her anger or to aspire to forgive her former husband, and she certainly does not feel she forfeits what Father Neuhaus called the "sustaining community of the church" because she is still angry and unforgiving. She is one of many quietly unorthodox believers who do not realize the radical implications of their ideas.

The effect of reinterpreting dogma can be far less benign than in the case of Mary Margaret and her priest. Father Neuhaus had explained that Christians consider forgiveness essential, but that reconciliation, while always desirable as an ideal, is not essential in circumstances when, "In the exercise of prudential judgment, contact will lead to bad consequences." Spiritual advisers ignore this distinction with disturbing frequency, and the consequences are bad indeed.

For ex-Catholic Lisa Remington, following her parish priest's naïve counsel to maintain contact with her stepfather prolonged his sexual victimization of her and paralyzed her ability to fight back. This psychopathic man, a powerful and prominent local politician whom nobody suspected, had molested Lisa and her older sister since they were children. "I kept it secret because I was afraid he'd kill us or my mother," Lisa, now twenty-five, told me with an intensity that belied her homecoming-queen insouciance. "At seventeen, I finally stopped denying what had happened, had myself wired, and taped him admitting it. I sent him to jail, and then later I collected four thousand signatures to prevent him from early parole; without the tape no one would ever have believed me. He was a monster."

The religious advice Lisa got throughout high school prevented her from severing her tie with her tormenter, though he continued to abuse her. "I talked to my priest who knew the whole story. He said 'Be the bigger person, Lisa. Turn the other cheek. Faith is like a baseball team—either you're on or you're off.' Being involved in the church kept me in the relationship with him—they would say there's nothing your family can do that isn't forgivable. I cut him off at the same time I stopped attending Mass. I never would have freed myself if I had continued to follow the priest's advice."

Although Lisa does not imagine that her priest knowingly sanctioned sexual abuse—a misguided emphasis on a distorted notion of forgiveness and family values is not an endorsement of criminality—she feels that the self-abnegating attitude he preached contributed to her vulnerability and reinforced a dangerous tendency to consider everybody's needs but her own. "Until I brought my stepfather to trial I placated everyone. I had to be the peacemaker and keep people happy."

Lisa's stepfather still harasses her, but now she refuses to see him. "He keeps looking for me—I had to leave town and get an unlisted phone number to protect myself. And he still denies that this affected me at all. What he did was an unforgivable act." Any clergyman who advocates reconciliation under these conditions also commits an unforgivable act.

Reformed Forgivers

We tend to think of forgiveness as the best, healthiest way to resolve an intimate injury, and of learning to forgive as one of life's greatest lessons. Sometimes the opposite is true. Learning not to forgive, after a life in which forgiveness has been compulsive, imposed, or unconsidered, deserves praise. Considering the pressure people feel to believe that they must be forgiving to be good, choosing the alternative may be the harder task.

Daily life provides many circumstances where offensive and unchangeable behavior should not be excused and where forgiving is confused with submerging normal reactions to mistreatment. Even when the culprit is a peer and not a parent, and the injury is mundane, it can take years to stop extending infinite second chances.

Rita Bergman reversed her lifelong tendency to do what she was told when she turned seventy-five. "As I've grown older I've begun to think more about what I need. Screw it, I don't *have* to forgive anymore," she exclaimed.

The object of Rita's newfound insight was an old friend who had become so obnoxious and critical that she was offending everyone she knew. "I felt terribly sorry for her. She hasn't been the same person since she lost her husband and son a few years ago, and she's all alone." Repeated infuriating lunches, in which every aspect of her appearance was scrutinized and found wanting, made Rita vow to sever the tie, but she always ended up reconsidering for old time's sake. Only after Rita's closest friend refused to see her if this woman accompanied them did Rita realize enough was enough, stopped making the dates she had come to dread, and ended the relationship.

As with more serious injustices, understanding the source of someone's inexcusable behavior—even feeling sympathy for her plight—does not justify endless exposure to it; there is a fine line between compassion and compliance. "I don't believe in carrying grudges at this point in my life," Rita said, "but how long could I continue to ignore my own feelings? I was always very timid and never opened my mouth, but now that has changed." Rita's refusal to overlook her unfortunate friend's hostility any longer is an act of self-respect that took a lifetime to attain.

Forgiving without reconciling is acceptable; why not reconciling without forgiving? People often wound one another in the name of truth; they may also deploy judicial dishonesty to protect themselves against pointless emotional onslaughts.

Sarah Goodman recently reversed her pattern of placating her older sister Wendy. Stricken with a rare cancer in childhood, married to a repugnant layabout, Wendy has lived a life of bad luck and bad judgment. Sarah's duties as the "good" daughter included overlooking Wendy's rages and insults in childhood, and not objecting when as an adult Wendy refused to help care for their dying father. "I was the one who was always pressured to do the right thing," Sarah said. "That was my script. I'd give in to keep the peace, but I can't and won't do it anymore; her problems are not my fault, and the way she vanished when our father got sick was inexcusable. I used to cry and curse her; now I'm civil. I'm no longer capable of forgiving her, whether she deserves it or not."

Sarah's cordiality toward her sister, which she maintains for their mother's sake, is a conscious pretense on her part and her best defense; she has decided that confrontation is too costly. "It never worked in the past, and now if I tell her how I feel I'll be punished. I don't wish her harm, but I want nothing to do with her on an emotional level."

Sarah frankly admits she derives secret pleasure from no longer turning the other cheek in the privacy of her own heart. Her customized solution involves a measure of hypocrisy, without self-delusion.

Unforgiving reconciliation is an ethical form of retribution. Like other responsible types of unforgiveness, it provides relief, closure, and insight. "At my father's funeral I saw what a miserable person she was, a tormented soul who hasn't connected to anybody, " Sarah recalled with more sadness than satisfaction. "I feel that really wonderful sense of indifference you have when you break up with somebody and you think you'll never get over the pain, and then one day you bump into each other on the street and wonder how you ever felt that way." Refusing to be what Lisa Remington's priest would call "the bigger person" freed Sarah to be her own person.

The Vengeful

I once had a patient who enthusiastically regaled me with the contents of a vicious anonymous letter she sent to a woman who had humiliated her years before. Hearing her grim and rapturous depiction of how her enemy must have suffered when she opened the envelope repelled me. Why, I wondered, did the spectacle of her satisfied lust disturb me so? Because I envied it, even as I saw how it

dehumanized her. I would never permit myself to experience, let alone act on, the taboo desire that she carried
out without apparent discomfort. Knowing that I, too,
could think of people to whom I might want to send such
a letter—though I'm not sure mine would be anonymous—that I, too, could imagine enjoying the crushed
look on their faces in the brief interval before my conscience caught up with me, humbled me. What was my
turning away from my father when he was dying but
disavowed revenge? God would not have had to insist
that "vengeance is Mine" so vehemently were we not
sorely tempted to make it ours.

Everyone has twinges of desire for blood, especially
when a hurt is fresh, but the better socialized and less
desperate suppress it. I unconsciously envied my patient
for what appeared to be her freedom to express the forbidden, when in fact she was enslaved by a pitiless and
unsatisfiable wish to get even, rooted in helplessness and
rage. The obsessive rumination of the vengeful only resembles productive thinking; it endlessly retraces the
same wretched terrain, devoid of true reflection or of
hope.

Vengefulness bears little relation to rational unforgiveness. It more closely resembles false forgiveness. Both are
automatic, undiscriminating compulsions that foreclose
reengagement and destroy the possibility of real
resolution.

The vengeful never choose not to forgive; it consumes
them. To be in their company is to be among the possessed. The pseudoforgivers I interviewed could not wait
to change the subject; the vindictive ones could not stop
talking about it. Sam Nelson and Elaine Walker—both

thirty years old, and perfectly decent, intelligent, funny people outside the bounds of their obsession—started talking before I sat down and were still at it when I got up to leave. They told their stories with a relentlessness that induces annoyance rather than sympathy, and guiltlessly, even gleefully, said things that most people would be too ashamed to admit. Since neither of them is a psychopath or a dangerous paranoid, they confine themselves to wishing ill rather than plotting it. Even though they clearly had been mistreated in incidents that happened several years ago, their legitimate grievances seem lost in the all-encompassing hatred they exuded. They portray their betrayers—the gold-digging girlfriend who had been spectacularly unfaithful to him and the duplicitous boss who had unfairly fired her—not as petty or cruel human beings, but as monsters deserving destruction. Without knowing it, they confer superhuman status and extraordinary power on their "enemies." Their strenuous efforts to annihilate that power unwittingly perpetuated it; I had the feeling that Sam and Elaine themselves, rather than the culprits they thought they were pursuing, were the real prey.

These two people, who ostensibly had little in common—Sam came from a working-class Catholic background and Elaine was an upper-middle-class Jew—had similar demeanors, emotions, and opinions; preoccupation with their injuries and a lust for revenge had submerged their individuality. It had also narrowed their range; no topic outside their grievances, the infamy of their nemeses, and an overly detailed exegesis of what had befallen them held their interest. Elaine complained that friends had dropped her because she had lost her job and with it her professional identity; it never occurred to her that her obsession, rather than her employment status, had alienated them.

It particularly struck me that, despite all the time Sam and Elaine had devoted to thinking about their troubles, neither had ever tried to understand the personalities or the motives of their betrayers—a task that others who do not forgive work hard to do. Their state of mind prevented them from imagining any perspective but their own, any role but victim, and any goal but getting even.

"I certainly will never forgive my boss—ever," Elaine insisted vociferously, as though the very idea were anathema. "There's no room for compromise on this," echoed Sam. "When somebody deliberately and maliciously does you wrong, forgiving facilitates it; that's allowing people to get over on you."

Their unequivocal rejection of the very idea of forgiveness sounds superficially like what moral unforgivers say; the difference is that Sam and Elaine make no exceptions. Sam, who has more self-awareness and perspective than Elaine, recognizes his prejudice. "My nickname in the army was 'Angry Sam.' I carry grudges like luggage. When I look at my life to see whom I've forgiven, the answer is nobody." Elaine, who was more preoccupied with the details of her summary dismissal—she supplied the exact date, time, and a verbatim account of the proceedings—does believe she made peace with her hypercritical mother in the past, but since she described her as a "terribly twisted woman whose model of child rearing was Nazi boot camp," her claim is suspect. "I still walk down the street muttering at my boss," she said. "I think about her every day. How can she live with herself after what she did to me? I got screwed, and there's nothing I can do."

I asked Sam why he could not imagine forgiving anybody who hurt him. "That would mean it doesn't bother me and I'm able to go on," he explained. "I'd have to rehash the whole thing in my head; why should I take the trouble?" He could not imagine any benefit for him in reexperiencing his pain and was astonished when I told him that people can forgive for their own sake, sometimes even after the perpetrator's death.

Two characteristics make the vengeance obsessed unable to resolve their injuries: unwillingness to reengage with the experience and an unexamined, unbearable sense of helplessness. Intimate injury assaults self-esteem, upsets the order of one's world, and creates or abets intense feelings of impotence. Shame, rage, and the wish to retaliate are its natural, universal consequences. People who lack resilience and the resources to metabolize it, which takes time in the best of circumstances, try to undo their devastation by projecting their hostility onto the betrayer. This makes them feel persecuted as well as betrayed and justifies retaliatory measures. Then the victim becomes, at least temporarily, the victimizer and—as the priest and the rabbi declared on *Good Morning America*—"evil is recycled" ad infinitum.

One of the ways to turn the tables is to imagine gruesome fates befalling those who have harmed you, and to take pleasure in imagining harming them in return. Sam said, "I consider my ex-girlfriend like the Nazis or the Ebola virus. If I could do her physical harm I would. I'm not proud of this, but I've heard her life isn't so smooth and I chuckle." Elaine was even more graphic: "If I heard that somebody had slashed my boss's face I'd smile, but"—she added as a disclaimer—"I wouldn't do it myself. If I found out she were dying I'd go out and celebrate; I wouldn't mind if her boyfriend gave her HIV." They both feel entirely justified and guiltless because, they rationalize, they are only doing unto others what has been done to them. Forgiveness may not necessarily beget more forgiveness, but vengeance always feeds on itself.

Why are Elaine and Sam possessed by emotions that most of us eventually get over? Their histories and their personalities make them more vulnerable. Both had violent, authoritarian parents who crushed their children's wills and treated them like objects: Elaine a "Nazi boot camp" mother and Sam a sadistic policeman father whom he still hates and "has no plans" to pardon. Certain family configurations predispose children to react to violation with a vengeance. The intensity and duration of an individual's response is determined not by the gravity of the injury alone, but by what it means in the context of a life.

Plotting revenge makes the powerless feel momentarily powerful, although it never works for long and has to be repeated endlessly. Evening the score is only an illusion; what was done can never be undone, so the perpetrator still wins. Sam's girlfriend's misery or Elaine's boss's mutilation would not heal or remove the psychic hurt that had already been inflicted; without insight, the wounds would continue to fester. Only the hard work of reengagement, recognition, and grieving softens the scar betrayal leaves behind.

Vengeance must not be confused with legitimate unforgiveness, a vast domain populated by ethical, responsible people rather than hate-filled wretches bent on retribution. Forgiveness and unforgiveness are not polar opposites but points on a continuum. The same internal processes can lead to emotionally authentic resolutions in either direction. Anyone who has gone through the profound and punishing process of conscious forgiving *or* not forgiving emerges more self-aware, more related to others, and less burdened by the past.

When it is genuine, forgiveness is a capacity not a compulsion; this is why the same person can grant it or withhold it, depending on the circumstances. The ability to discriminate signifies maturity and freedom.

Mme de Stael was wrong; understanding need not lead to forgiveness—but it can lead to wisdom.

11

The Eye of the Beholder

BETRAYAL, like beauty, is in the eye of the beholder. Who you are determines what you see and what you make of it. The same behavior one person finds intolerable and devastating hardly matters to another. The subjective factor in forgiveness is so powerful that it actually helps create what people experience, subliminally coloring their perceptions and influencing their emotional reactions. This affects not only situations where the truth is ambiguous, but even so seemingly factual a matter as whether something happened or not. What gets edited out, or emphasized, depends on your perspective and your relationship to the perpetrator. There is no objective scale for weighing crimes of the heart.

Recognizing that it is up to the individual whether something registers as a betrayal—and whether or not something is forgivable—does not make that action less damaging or less worthy of condemnation, nor does it absolve the perpetrator of responsibility. It does mean that forgiveness can never be divorced from its context, uniformly packaged, or imposed.

The Charming Professor

I met dapper, renowned Prof. Max Mihaly in 1970, when I was a first-year graduate student and he was chairman of the psychology department. I heard that he was directing a research project on sleep and dreaming, and, since the topic fascinated me and I needed a job, I swallowed my trepidation and made an appointment to see him.

There in his office sat a bright-eyed, sprightly man around sixty, his high forehead, mane of graying chestnut hair, and signature bow tie wreathed in the smoke of a thousand Gitanes. When he stood and bowed to me with European suavity I was surprised at how slight he was; his electric energy and aura of lightly carried erudition made him seem much larger. Casting furtive glances at the handsome smoking paraphernalia and antiques scattered among his old adding machines and the stacks of books and journals in assorted languages, I managed to introduce myself. "I really want to do research," I said. "You're hired," he replied. Thus I became, for the second time in my life, the "little assistant" to a man whose compelling brilliance and generosity coexisted with chilling, reckless amorality.

Dr. Mihaly's romantic exploits were legendary at the university and seemed as much a part of him as his dashing wardrobe and nearly impenetrable accent. In the decade I worked for him I watched a steady stream of smart and stunning women of all ages stop in to visit him. He embraced them all, and they all adored him. Once early in our relationship he extended a desultory amorous invitation to me as well, but he accepted my demurral gracefully and never repeated it during the twenty-five years I knew him. He gave me full credit on every joint project (a rare courtesy in academia), approved of my husband, and enthusiastically encouraged my professional development. So inspiring was his verve, intellectual curiosity, and physical resilience in old age, that I found it hard to believe when I learned that he had died in his late eighties.

Over the years, I came to know the other surrogate daughter in Max's life, his secretary Robin Brown, who ran his busy psychotherapy office. I also met Max's two sons—Thomas, the elder, whose relationship with his father had always been combative and who had himself become a psychologist of a diametrically opposite persuasion, and Eugene, the younger, who was close to his father and embodied his bohemian side.

One of Max's many professional responsibilities was chairing the committee that monitored the professional conduct of psychotherapists in the region, a duty he took very seriously and often discussed with me. He was scandalized by colleagues who dared to have sex with their patients—his own dalliances would never violate so sacred a trust—and justifiably proud of the disciplinary actions he spearheaded against offenders. His zeal impressed me, and I agreed with it; I too considered patient-therapist sex a particularly malign variation on incest.

Soon after his death, Robin called to tell me that a woman whom she herself had referred to Max long ago had confessed to her that he had been sleeping with her for years, as had, she subsequently discovered, many of his other women patients. Horrified, Robin immediately told Max's sons and took it upon herself to write a letter resigning him from the ethics committee. Like me, she had grudgingly accepted Max's other infidelities, but this violation made her feel so outraged and personally betrayed that she could hardly contain herself; she found his behavior absolutely unforgivable.

Although I sympathized with her point of view, I did not share it. His offense, while objectively worse than my father's, was outside the context of our relationship; I myself had never sent him a patient. Max's hypocrisy and psychopathy were disturbingly familiar to me, but since I was not his daughter—nor his unwitting procurer—I judged him rather than hated him. Perhaps my already having come to terms with the same flaw in my father's character contributed to my relative equanimity.

Along with throngs of admirers, Robin, Tom, Gene, and I attended Max's memorial service with disparate sets of emotions. Gene spoke easily and glowingly of the wonderful adventures he shared with his father; Tom, struggling to be fair, praised his achievements but alluded to his "dark side"; and I, despite my revulsion at what I had recently learned about him, paid tribute to his influence on my life. Robin wept but could not bring herself to eulogize him.

Afterward, I asked each of them to describe the reactions evoked by this remarkable man who had committed inexcusable offenses. "They say you should forgive and forget," said Robin, "but I'm never going to forgive Max for this. It really threw me; he was like a father to me; I thought he was the end-all. I confronted him when I found out—'Did you fuck every single patient you had?'

I yelled. I wrote a letter of resignation for him, signed his name, and told him I'd sent it, which he never reacted to. After that our relationship changed and I was always angry at him; I kept my distance because I despised his values. I loved him, but he was impossible."

As furious as she still was over Max's breech, Robin could not forget her admiration or their mutual devotion, and she felt anguish about her inability to reconcile her contradictory emotions. "He always supported me, particularly after my own father died," she recalled. "He was there through every tragedy. And he triumphed over so much in his own life—near-fatal illnesses, running from the Communists. He was so complex and so needy, so fascinating and such a pain in the ass. He knew what society demanded, but never abided by the rules in any area of his life; he made himself the exception." This, she knew, was the key to his originality as well as his destructive selfishness.

Robin was taken aback when I asked her whether Max resembled her father. "They were so similar that I didn't even see it. Both of them had a great facade, and both were fun, inquisitive, charming, and talented; they seemed secure but were deeply insecure. I was too young to have a dialogue with my father, who died when I was twenty-eight, so I communicated with Max as I never could with him."

Despite her disillusionment—"I'll never refer a woman to a male therapist again, and I've become less trusting in general," she said—Robin likes the way she handled Max. "Confronting him made my whole life different. I learned not to sit on anger. He came off his pedestal—I'm more honest than he was, and I don't live a double standard like he did. Now I know who I am, and I'm proud of myself. Something good came from something bad."

Why was Robin's reaction more intense than mine? Though Max's personality shared elements with both our fathers, whom we lost at about the same age, his lifelong adolescent brashness made him resemble hers more closely; she had once described her father to me as "Peter Pan." Max also played a more central role in Robin's life; she relied on him and really recreated a father-daughter relationship with him. In contrast, my position exposed me to more of his virtues and shielded me from his vices. Because I was not implicated and felt no responsibility for his most outrageous escapades, I had more distance; he was my intellectual mentor, not my emotional anchor. Betrayal affects you more when you have more to lose.

Robin never pardoned Max's lapse because it was too major a violation of her beliefs, but she did come to accept that the contradictions of his character, and the ambivalence he engendered, could never fully to be resolved. Though she would not expose Max publicly in his lifetime, she punished him and prevented him from committing further abuses of power. The disciplinary measures she took restored her good opinion of herself and expiated any lingering feelings of guilt she felt for having referred the patient in the first place. Robin's appropriate satisfaction at her own moral superiority was a theme repeated by many others who had been betrayed by those whom they had formerly admired—Sophia Agnoletti's playboy father, David Darielle's exacting lover. Their sentiments provide consolation even as they wreak just vengeance.

Some months later, I talked to Dr. Thomas Mihaly,

Max's older son, who had come to resemble his father uncannily now that he himself was the age Max was when we first met. He had always struck me as more solid, more outwardly reserved yet more genuinely accessible, than his quicksilver father. How, I wondered, had Robin's disclosure affected his already tarnished image of the man I still esteemed? "It's pretty far down on the list, considering everything else he did to me" was, I thought, a strangely muted reaction for any clinician, let alone the son of a psychologist who had violated the prime directive of their mutual profession. "I'd always suspected he'd done it, but when she told me about the affairs he had with patients, I didn't want to hear it," he admitted. "I said, 'Who knows what the truth really is?'"

Tom's next statement shocked and saddened me more than what Robin had revealed about Max. "I had my own reasons not to want to be faced with what my father did; I had an affair with a patient myself about twenty years ago—I must have been pretty psychotic at the time. We moved in together for a year, and I was convinced I wanted to marry her. I've always had a tendency not to think about things but to live them out, just like he did." I was appalled and pained to see the lengths this decent man and caring therapist had gone to identify with and to understand his unreachable parent, how he had unconsciously competed on Max's own forbidden turf; he was even on an ethics committee himself at the time. "I remember being fascinated when my father bragged about women," he said. "It made him a real man in my eyes."

The son dealt with the consequences of his own deed in a radically different way than his father had. "Several years afterward, I went to the ethics committee on my own and said 'I'm tired of acting as though my affair didn't happen.' Then I told the story to students as a cautionary tale. It was shameful; the more I talked the more sickened and horrified I was that I could have done it." Unlike Max, whom Robin had called "the king of denial," his heir abdicated the throne.

Tom tried to talk to Max about their shameful secrets. "After I found out what he had done, I attempted to discuss it with him once when we were alone before he died; he denied everything. I felt really disappointed, because I wasn't there to blame him. I saw that he couldn't do anything different; he couldn't be honest. It disturbs me how little integrity he had." Like Robin, Tom discerned the weakness behind Max's bravado and appreciated his own moral superiority. "I realized he was defensive, vulnerable, and fragile—and I saw how much better I've done by going public and making people understand the temptation." Confessing and confronting the truth expiated the guilt that had oppressed him for years and helped him finally separate from his father.

Tom also did something else his father would have considered unthinkable and unnecessary; he decided to reenter intensive psychotherapy. "I had a hard time when he died; I was just angry. At his funeral I didn't want to hear from anybody what a great guy he was, but three months later at his memorial I could listen to the appreciation and know how important he was to so many people." Tom's outrage gave way to compassion and a sense of loss when he began to grieve for what he never had. "It was hard to identify with him because he never made room for me; he preempted all the space. All my life I tried to make myself as small as possible to avoid his wrath. I could never trust him or open my heart—I could never even fight with him like my brother could. Now I'm sorry that we didn't have a better relationship—although I did become a psychologist like him. I understand now that he was limited; he's wounded and so am I. When I could see his wounds, I began to miss him." Max, always an oversize figure, became human to his son for the first time.

Meeting with Tom's younger brother Eugene Mihaly was like encountering an entirely different, but just as unmistakable, image of their father. Gene, an urban planner with the familiar penetrating, dancing eyes and breezy charm, embodied Max's brash, eternally youthful side. I heard another version of events from him.

According to Gene, he never had to pardon his father because he never felt betrayed or even upset with Max during his lifetime. "When Robin wrote me about his affair with his patient he was already dead, so I never developed strong angry feelings about it. I can't forgive him if I never felt resentment." Gene said this not because he took his father's misconduct lightly; in fact, he took it so seriously that he literally had to hide the evidence from himself. "Her letter was pretty painful to read, so I filed it in a drawer. I was very secretive and didn't show it to anybody. It was damning, actually—he really took advantage of a vulnerable person—and it felt so ironic that he taught courses on ethics. I must have thought, 'It's so heavy, I'll just fold this letter back up and put it in its envelope and look at it a few years from now.' "

There was only one problem with Gene's account: Since Robin told me that she had informed both brothers simultaneously, he had actually learned of his father's conduct before, not after, his death. His need to maintain an untainted relationship with Max compelled him not only to conceal the truth, but unwittingly to alter the sequence of events retrospectively.

Robin's letter was not the first piece of upsetting data Gene "filed." "My dad and I just resolved things," he explained. "Tom was always angry with him, but none of that stuff registered with me, except for one little thing."

The "little thing" was one I had witnessed in my own life when I was a few years younger than he, with consequences that could not have been more different. "I first suspected something was going on when I showed up unexpectedly at age twenty-two while my mother was in Europe. He was giving a party at the house with someone else. I flashed on the scene in *Death of a Salesman* where the son experiences a devastating exposure to his father's affair. We never discussed it—the typical male way of dealing with things. My father asked me not to tell my mother, and I never did. I buried the incident; it's had little effect on my relationship with him. Maybe I cut him a lot of slack. Maybe it was so disturbing I never wanted to acknowledge it." With the classic logic of the false forgiver, he explained, "This was just something he was doing and I was disappointed; if he'd walked out on my mother and divorced her it would have been different. It wasn't like the person I saw was the other woman and it was ongoing." Perhaps Gene also cultivated tolerance because he secretly relished the role of favored coconspirator and confidant that he knew he had with his father and his brother did not.

Gene combines insight and obliviousness. Periodically he registers what he denies, but does it anyway. "Maybe

I'm operating on automatic instead of dealing with this in a more conscious way," he admitted. "I don't let myself recognize the meaning of what he did, as opposed to saying 'I don't want to be like him.'" Taking in unsavory information about his beloved father could ruin everything.

While there is no question that Gene buried much of the impact of Max's misconduct, their special bond also genuinely lessened the brunt of Max's character flaws. Since Max could "make room" for his younger son as he never could for his elder, Gene felt not betrayed but included; siblings do not have the same psychological parents even though they share the same biological ones. Gene viewed his father in an entirely different light from Max's elder son, his secretary, or his protégée—the light of idealized, unconditional love and natural affinity. He genuinely had less to forgive than his brother had.

Professor Mihaly's two sons and two "daughters" dealt with his breech of ethics in radically different ways; Robin condemned his behavior, Tom acted it out, Gene denied it, and I accepted it. Each of us viewed him from our unique perspective and interpreted his conduct in the context of our histories and our relationships with him. We created the lenses through which we perceived him, and those lenses registered four distinct, though related, images. I mentioned this to Robin, who agreed that the phenomenon is as ubiquitous as it is disconcerting. "The same thing happened after my father died," she said. "When my two brothers and I sat down to talk about him, we discovered that we were talking about three different men—and I'd never met the other two."

Lady Luck

Two boys grew up in neighboring New Jersey industrial towns in the fifties. Both came from working-class Italian families, won scholarships, and eventually became psychotherapists. Both were also sons of compulsive gamblers, whose disastrous impulsiveness and chronic debts forced their families to live in depressingly similar atmospheres of chaos and dread. One son admires and emulates his father; the other despises and despairs over his.

"I never even thought that forgiveness was relevant to him until you brought it up," said Vince Cavalli, a lithe, black leather–jacketed fifty-year-old who talked fast and well and retained an air of street smarts. "My father's so easy to forgive—it's simple and clear-cut. All my life I've treated his behavior only as something I needed to understand; I never took it personally. When he borrowed my student loan, or lost the last bit of money we had, it was like an alcoholic taking a drink; he wasn't trying to hurt his son. I know that he would have spent the money on us had he won. He was an extremely generous person, so it all balanced out." Only when I pressed him did I discover that Vince's father never repaid the loan money he "borrowed."

As reasonable as it sounded on the surface, Vince's explanation for his lack of resentment against his father struck me as odd. Was the disregard of an alcoholic or a gambler for the lives of everyone around him any less devastating or reprehensible because it was not directed specifically at his son? Since I have treated several gamblers' children as patients, I am grimly familiar with the havoc their parents' habit always wreaks, the humiliation and anxiety that undermine basic security and typically take years to undo. Vince's reaction, like that of other false forgivers, seemed short-circuited at best. Had he miraculously erased his fury at his father or managed somehow never to feel betrayed in the first place?

Vince did not deny what he called "the dark side" of his father's obsession; he spun it out of existence. He also glossed over his father's violence toward him, his repeated thefts of Vince's savings, and his mob connections as though they were the most minor and effortlessly pardonable of infractions. "Even though it seemed like the end of the world—I always thought they'd shut the electricity off or throw us out on the street—nothing bad ever really happened. My father must have won a lot—he wasn't that bad a gambler." His logic sounded like the excuses Gene Mihaly made for Max.

Accentuating the positive was Vince's means of survival as well as his philosophy of life. "I had to know what mood my father was in not to get beaten up, but it really paid off. Since I had to learn about him, I became very perceptive. Every time something bad happened I tried to turn it into something positive; you can't weigh that stuff too heavily. I solved the problem, and it became how I see the world." With a striking mixture of realism and rationalization, in language that disconnected the man from his actions, he said, "The gambling problem was just there, like cold in the winter; it was a fact of life."

Gambling is still a fact of Vince's life. "I inherited my father's genetic ability. I'm a gambler myself, though I'm not compulsive like he was. A compulsive gambler is out of control; to me it's a hobby. I gamble as often as possible—I've gone two, three days without sleeping—but never a lot of money. I'm a professional; I think of myself as a 'probabilities engineer.' "

Vince became defensive and annoyed when I suggested that preferring gambling to sleeping qualified as more than a hobby. Bets, he insisted, only make life more exciting, and he tried to point out the ways that everybody else did the same thing. Thus he converted childhood disaster to adult pleasure, turned insecurity into stimulation and a reason for living; why life did not feel sufficiently exciting without gambling he never considered. Like an amalgam of the Mihaly brothers, Vince idealized his father, identified with him, and copied him, all the while denying that anything bad had happened.

One of the reasons Vince went to such lengths to vindicate his father was that his mother was worse. "It's much, much more difficult to forgive her," Vince said, with a tone of bitter coldness absent when he spoke of his father. "Her behavior was more personal. She always compared me to my more successful cousin. When I opened my therapy office, she said I should have only five business cards printed because I would never make it, and she suggested I get a job as highway toll collector for security after I received my Master's degree. Because of her, I never thought I could accomplish anything." His mother's malicious criticism and undermining, which were directed expressly at him, were far more harmful than the inadvertent though more dramatic damage his father caused. "If my father went out and spent the rent money, who cared, but my mother said, 'You got ninety on the test and your cousin Eddy got ninety-five.' Even though it wasn't *Father Knows Best,* he and I were very close, and I always felt that in a perverted way he loved me." Intent to harm when she had the capacity to do otherwise made his mother more culpable in her son's eyes. Vince could not define his father's gambling as evil because he did not identify with his mother and the pain it caused her. He clung to his father's genuine virtues and minimized his vices in order to have at least one parent to love.

Frank Verdi—slender, serious and esthetic—was as raw as Vince was glib. For Frank, his own father's gambling was not a fact of life, but a catastrophe. "I can't forgive him—that's the starting point," he told me. "I can't even conceive of it. I like to think I'm reasonably mature and well-analyzed and what comes with that territory is you're supposed to 'let go'—isn't that the lingo?—of the dark past and move on. There's a dialectic of blame and forgiveness in my head, but I can't plot a path from one to the other. It makes me feel orphaned, although in some way I'm also orphaning my parents."

As part of his effort to come to terms with his history, Frank recently telephoned his father, who had sworn that he had given up gambling long ago, and got a repulsively familiar plea for cash. "He complained frantically about his predicament, and when I tried to advise him, he said, 'The only thing that's gonna help is money.' This was the same old gambler's logic, so I knew he'd never really quit. He hadn't reformed at all—my hope blew up in my face. I thought that he had gotten better, as I have. I felt like an inadequate son again, and also shocked, disappointed, and enraged. The whole relationship's been a cheat," he said with as much sorrow as bitterness. Vince prided himself on having "inherited" his father's betting instincts; Frank berated himself because his own optimism seemed like a parody of his father's delusion that his luck would always change tomorrow.

What made this encounter particularly excruciating is that his father's reaction reminded Frank of himself; he too shared the paternal weakness, going on spending sprees he could ill afford, though he handled it better. "I've squandered a lot of money over the years; the sin of the father has been my sin. My connection to him is a burden and a source of shame. Now I have only a little more debt to pay off; I'm taking care of my messy past. Some days I'm proud of how far I've come, and others I'm walking around with the mark of Cain, terrified that I'm just like him. Having money problems myself is my way not to lose him, not to pass him by; it has defined my life." Resembling his father is anything but a source of pride for Frank. The sorrow that engulfs him is essential to the task of mourning in which he is engaged. Vince, who explains it away, is still under its spell.

Horrors that must have been just as common in the Cavalli household were far more obviously damaging to the Verdis' son. "People used to call my mother and threaten that she'd never see us again unless my father paid off 'the shylocks.' I thought they must be some kind of horrible monsters that were going to kill him. I used to get what I called my 'disaster feeling' when their door would be shut, voices would be raised, and he'd disappear for days. I adored him as a little boy; I was horrified of losing him. Talking about it reminds me of how lunatic it was, and how sad."

One reason Frank's feelings about his father are so different from Vince's is that Frank was extremely close to his mother, so that his reactions were colored by hers.

"I was totally identified with her, so I shared her devastation. It was like a lightning bolt when I finally realized that she got something out of the situation, that martyrdom appealed to her." Vince always felt that his father loved and approved of him, but as Frank grew older, his father began to behave more like Vince's mother, deriding him and belittling his interests in art and literature. This left his son with an unfulfilled longing for a man he could truly admire. "I never see anything in the media about fathers and sons that doesn't make me burst into tears with utter immediacy. I'm hungry to be loved by a father—it's a real lack, an ache and piece of emptiness I carry with me all the time. I'm looking for an older male mentor to fill the role—perhaps an editor." As for his own father, "When he dies I'll only feel dull regret. The best I can hope for is to disengage." To face the truth about his father has meant losing him as a role model, but finding his own separate, and far saner, identity.

Every beholder has a different pair of eyes, which see a selective piece of reality. Sexual misconduct and compulsive gambling are objectively unconscionable acts, but only certain people subjectively define them as betrayals. Since there can be no universal standard for betrayal, neither can there be for forgiveness.

12

The Good Enough Life

WE need a more forgiving definition of forgiveness—
one more attuned to human limitation, more flexible, and
more compassionate. The work of resolving betrayal is
difficult enough without the additional burden of believing, as so many people do, that you must extirpate all
traces of anger, bitterness, or resentment to qualify as a
genuinely forgiving person. Forgiveness is the rebirth of
positive emotions, not the wholesale obliteration of negative ones. Ambivalence permeates our ongoing relationships with people we love; how can it be missing with
people we forgive?

The doctrine of universal forgiveness is one-size-fits-
all absolutism. Encouraging people to strive for this unrealistic goal—even when the motive is salvaging their psy-
ches or saving their souls—instills needless feelings of
inadequacy in anyone who fails to achieve it. Worse, it
encourages false forgiveness, which threatens to inundate
our public as well as our private lives. The question "Does

this person deserve to be forgiven and am I able to do it?'' should not be taboo. To insist on forgiveness in all cases is to confuse forgiving with resolving, to equate unforgiveness with vengefulness, and to ignore the critical role subjectivity plays in determining what is forgivable and what is not.

The pediatrician-psychoanalyst D. W. Winnicott's concept of the "good enough mother" provides an alternative. The kind of parent Winnicott had in mind makes plenty of mistakes. She fails—sometimes even hates—her child, but her heart is mostly in the right place. To strive to be "good enough" forgivers, to come to terms as best we can with our betrayers, is all we can expect. There are no perfect acts of forgiveness because there are no perfect people. Forgiveness is about recognizing the humanity and the limitations of the other; the person doing the forgiving deserves the same consideration.

Both religious and secular advocates of universal forgiveness fail to recognize that forgiveness and nonvengeful unforgiveness are points on a continuum, not qualitatively different, unrelated processes. Under certain circumstances, the refusal to forgive is just as mature and accomplishes many of the same goals. Valid forms of resolution are as various as the individuals who achieve them. The emotional authenticity of a solution is the only legitimate criterion for judging it.

The portrait of forgiveness that emerges from the stories my subjects told me is neither serene nor simple. Even those who literally fell into the arms of their former enemies continued to be troubled by past hurts from time to time. Rare is the deep wound that leaves no scar when it heals.

Hostility is a neglected and much-maligned component of forgiveness, as well as of most other human enter-
prises. Those who have truly forgiven may on occasion
gloat, get furious, feel superior, or enjoy the satisfaction
of being successful when their betrayers fail, or alive
when their betrayers are dead. Such emotions do not con-
taminate compassion; in healthy forms and manageable
doses, they accompany it and even facilitate it. I find that
my patients who are best acquainted with their aggression
are the ones least likely to live it out unawares.

In addition to the assumption that hostility is foreign
to the forgiving heart, three other myths distort our understanding of the process: that it is completeable, that it
is consistent, and that it is under conscious control.

My own experience contradicts all these notions. Although I believe I have made considerable progress in
forgiving my father, I expect to go on doing it, discovering
new aspects of it, for the rest of my life. Sometimes even
now, when something a patient says or a story in the
news reminds me of the anguish he caused me, I am disturbed or disgusted all over again. I will probably always
be overly sensitive, and too harshly judgmental, about du-
plicity and sexual betrayal, particularly when children get
caught in the crossfire. This does not stop me from feeling
delighted when my husband wears one of my father's
ties, or nostalgic when I hear the music he loved. I still
weep every time I read "The Nightingale," and my reaction always takes me by surprise. I understand that neither my mourning nor my recoiling at what we both did
will ever end because they will always be part of who
I am.

I never set out to forgive my father, and doubtless

would have rebelled if anybody had suggested that I should; trying to override my negative emotions before I understood them would have recapitulated my earlier desperate and dangerous defenses. And even if I had tried to will myself to do it, no amount of effort would have succeeded until maturity and life experience made me capable. However, in retrospect, I see how natural and almost inevitable the outcome was given what I *did* seek to do—which was to know our relationship more deeply. By doing the emotional work of reengaging, recognizing, and reinterpreting, and most of all by being willing to take responsibility for my part, I created a psychic state of receptivity in which new feelings could grow. I did not need, and would have been hampered by, a more prescribed course of action. That I forgave him in my own way and in my own time makes my action most precious, and most authentic. I know that this is what he would have wanted.

Forgiving my father was by no means a foregone conclusion or the only acceptable outcome, and I could not have done so if the circumstances of my life had not been conducive to it. My own effort would have allowed me to resolve (at least to some extent)—to reengage with, recognize, and reinterpret—my feelings about our relationship, but not necessarily to forgive his betrayal of me. And that would have been all right.

There is no such thing as an objectively forgivable betrayal because feelings occur in the context of a relationship and the rest of a life. What love there was, and how much can be recovered, determines the outcome; will alone cannot.

Even a resolutely planned conscious act of forgiveness,

like Tammy Kaye's or Rachel Sachs's or Sophia Agno-letti's, is less rational than it appears—and, as Jackie O'Connor discovered, making forgiveness your goal does not guarantee results. Forgiveness can no more be created by fiat than love can; effort and intent only prepare the internal environment for nature to take its course. Recognizing the unconscious component in every act of forgiveness allows us to focus on the process of resolution rather than its outcome, and helps us learn to tolerate the ambiguity and anxiety necessary for profound personal change. In contrast, affirmations like "I want to be better, not bitter," which one forgiveness instruction manual recommends, seek to legislate and forcibly overcome emotions, not live in them. Formulas impose a predetermined direction, which is more likely to produce false forgiveness than the real thing. Exhortation is no substitute for self-examination, and the only one who has the right to determine the proper outcome is the person who has been betrayed.

As a psychotherapist, I have learned that setting agendas for others is a tricky business, more likely to reflect my own bias than the patient's genuine needs. Compliance can easily be mistaken for change. The more open-ended, personalized goal of the good enough resolution encourages people to think and feel for themselves, with the assurance that what they accomplish will suffice.

"I'd never even consider forgiving my parents," a patient of mine told me emphatically. I neither applauded his refusal nor exhorted him to change his mind. All I asked was what forgiving them meant to him. "I'd have to see their importance, my dependence, their power over me, how they made me and deformed me, and how my love turned to hate," he replied. My job is to help him "see," understand, and feel everything he enumerated as fully as possible. I cannot predict, and do not care, whether doing so will lead him to forgive his parents, only that he break their spell—and forgive himself.

If forgiveness is not the goal, what does a good enough resolution of intimate betrayal consist of? Seeing what happened to you, and seeing it clearly. Trying to discover your own part in creating and perpetuating the situation—what Jack O'Reilly called "looking in the mirror"—and facing this no matter how hard it is, or how hideous the reflection seems. Grieving for the losses you have sustained, whether the relationship has any redeeming features to recover or not. Accepting that the pain will be a permanent, though not dominant, part of your life. Making sincere efforts to grasp the reality of your betrayer. Accepting uncertainty and ambivalence. Allowing for radical revisions of your understanding as life changes you. Not deciding in advance where the process must take you, but trusting that you will get there. Cultivating the capacity to forgive, avoiding the compulsion to exercise it indiscriminately, and applying your knowledge to yourself.

If, like Christopher Young, we can eventually say "poor man" about a father who beats and humiliates us, even if we still fight with him internally and wish we had had a different father, we have said the most important thing. If, like Dana Reinhardt and Jessica Kramer, we can understand but can never love a mother who hated us and not helplessly recapitulate that terrible tie, we have liberated ourselves. If, like Jonathon Bishop, we are torn between outrage and the wish for peace our whole lives, we are only human.

I still have not visited my father's grave—but I did reopen the door to his office; that was the place I knew I needed to go. Since several people assumed that now, "for closure," I would want to see where he was buried and were surprised that I hadn't made the trip, I asked myself why I had stopped short of what seemed the ultimate, "natural" resolution. Was I avoiding something I should be confronting? Was I still angry, rebellious, secretly withholding, stubbornly refusing to take "the next step"? Was I denying the reality of his death? After much consideration, I came to a different conclusion: I have not gone there because it is not the proper place for me to remember him.

For me, visiting his grave because it is supposed to be the "right" thing to do would provide only an artificial and external notion of resolution, the kind of empty gesture he does not deserve. Because the motivation to go there does not come from within, it feels inauthentic for me. I want nothing false in my forgiveness.

My choice would not be right for everyone. For someone else, a grave might represent a concrete presence, a focus for feeling, a place to contemplate the meaning of a life. My memories have different sites, which are just as powerful for me; a grave is not where I would go to commune with anyone I love who had died.

These were not always my reasons for not going. Originally my refusal was my ultimate way to reject and punish him—an extension of not ever wanting to see him again after he turned his back on me at the hospital, leaving the room while he wept the last time we were to-gether, and refusing to see him when he was dying. Because I no longer feel guilty about these actions, as much as I regret them, I don't have to prove I'm a good dutiful daughter—or disprove it by an empty act of piety that I'm a bad one.

Making peace is often a complicated, incomplete task, and inviolably personal. Individual truth, not premature closure or following external dictates, matters most. The resolution is more important than the form it takes. I am grateful that my not going to his grave reflects how I really feel and is no longer a repudiation of our relationship.

I do not plan to make the literal pilgrimage—although I have not foreclosed the possibility of a change of heart at some future time—because I do not believe his essence is to be found there. Bitterness and vindictiveness no longer hold me back; I visit him daily. I choose to sing the Nightingale's song not in a cemetery, but to his living presence in my life and in these pages.